Please God,
Don't Let My Badge Tarnish

Please God, Don't Let My Badge Tarnish

ONE MAN'S COURAGE TO TAKE A STAND!

KEVIN M. LACHAPELLE

iUniverse, Inc.
New York Lincoln Shanghai

Please God, Don't Let My Badge Tarnish
One Man's Courage To Take A Stand!

Copyright © 2006, 2007 by Kevin M. LaChapelle

iUniverse books may be ordered through booksellers or by contacting:

iUniverse
2021 Pine Lake Road, Suite 100
Lincoln, NE 68512
www.iuniverse.com
1-800-Authors (1-800-288-4677)

The views expressed in this work are solely those of the author and do not necessarily reflect the views of the publisher, and the publisher hereby disclaims any responsibility for them.

ISBN: 978-0-595-38238-5 (pbk)
ISBN: 978-0-595-82606-3 (cloth)
ISBN: 978-0-595-82604-9 (ebk)

Printed in the United States of America

Contents

Acknowledgement

I hope this book inspires readers to stand up for what they know is right no matter what the cost. I also hope the readers will realize how much opportunity they have to impact those around them everyday. For public officials, you have the opportunity to right wrongs everyday. For police officers, you have the opportunity to empower community member's each and every day you wear your uniform. We can never forget that if we cease having a positive impact on those around us, we become absolutely irrelevant. I for one never want my life to be irrelevant.

I want to thank my family first and foremost. They put up with my being the youngest and most annoying member of the family. For my Mom and Dad I am thankful for all they have taught me. For my Dad who taught me how to be innovative and find ways of fixing things. For my Mom who taught me to never lose faith in God and led by example in her love for putting others first. My oldest brother David for being a leader within our family and never being afraid to say what he knows needs to be said. To my oldest sister Leslie, for all she has endured in her life, which has given her so much compassion for others and the fact that she has so

much love for the downtrodden. She is a fighter and a survivor. I appreciate her so much for helping me layout this book. For my brother Brad who always offered such staunch protection for me during high school. His tenacity with his work and his always wanting to be there for others is an example to so many. For my twin sister Lyn who has been through it all. For her ability to finish nursing school and her commitment to ensure that the elderly patients under her care were always treated as she would like to be treated.

I have been so blessed by the friendships God has given to me. I especially want to thank Jose Orozco for all of his wisdom, inspiration and support. I thank Luis Martinez for all we have been through in our life and his steadfast willingness to be there always. I thank Carl Starrett for his steadfast friendship and never being afraid to tell me when I am wrong. I thank David Rios and Moises Fraire who stood by me in some of the lowest times ever. I thank Luis and Lucia Castillo, Lalo and Dara Gunther, Harley, Ryan, and Vanessa Gunther, Agustin Pena, Oscar Arce, James Velazquez, Jorge Briseno, Miguel and Ruby Samaniego, Jeff Cramer, Garry Gison, David Gastelum, Isidro Delgado, JD Moyer, Joe Sirard, Mike Bevis, Phanat Khammao, Thongwan Khammao, Viet and Aaron Hollenberg, Raul and Leti Flores, Sion Brannan, Tony Perez, Steve Gonzalez, Johnny Vo, and the many others who have had such profound impact on my life.

I thank my cousin Barbara Sheffield, Frank and Janis Osweiler, my mom, and the many others who proofread my manuscripts and offered their valuable input.

My hope while you read this book is not that you are awed at my abilities as a police officer, but rather how awesome the role of a police officer can be. A police officer can be a community hero, or become an irrelevant person who does nothing to empower people within their community. In this book you will see all of the incredible opportunities there are to impact those around you.

Interestingly, I hear so many people telling me how much of a blessing I am to them, when in fact they have no idea of the incredible blessing they actually are to me. I am so fortunate to have the multitudes of friends whom I cherish more than anything in my life. I find riches in friendships. In fact, with all that I endured, it was well worth it to have been able to meet all of the people over the years in which even today, I can call family!

Preface

As a means of introducing this book, I have asked a former police officer whom I did not know during my ordeal to introduce this book. He had quite a different perspective of who I was, but after having been enlightened as to what really happened, offers some interesting perspective and insight. In addition, I have asked my brother who was a police officer in a neighboring city to help in introducing this book.

Lance Ruiz, Former Police Officer, City of Coronado, California

It is a pleasure to be asked to contribute to this book. I want to provide a bit of insight as to the character of Kevin M. LaChapelle. He is a thoughtful, caring, and considerate person that has inspired many into greatness. All he demands is effort and he thrives on the passion for a cause. He listens to others for new ideas, gives them the credit they deserve and helps create and develop a shared vision towards well being. But that is not the Kevin I first learned about. I heard of an officer that was not a part of the brotherhood, falsely accused other officers of corruptness, and helped destroy a very popular police department. I would like to share the first memories I had of the events leading to the rumored history of Officer K. M. LaChapelle.

I was a rookie officer out of the "hard-core" town of Coronado. For those of you who are not familiar with the City of Coronado, it is the Beverly Hills of San Diego. Some people say it's La Jolla, but that just isn't true. I was young and thought I was well prepared to take on the world. For me, law enforcement was the ultimate compliment of a person. The characteristics that a police officer displays were one of honor, integrity and loyalty. This was instilled in me as a youngster handed down from my father. I was the kid in school that was so proud of his dad. I shared stories of my dad being a SWAT member for the United States Border Patrol. If you heard me then, you might think that my dad was the Federal Government and was able to protect and monitor our borders by himself. I might have embellished a story or two, but that just showed how proud I was of him. Since I was a youngster, I always knew what career I was bound for. To this day, I strongly believe the day I graduated from the police academy was the day that I paid my father back in full.

I remember parking at the station jumping out of my 1966 Ford Mustang and being the first one in the locker room. I would be the first one in the briefing room and already reading the pass down from other shifts. I had some great training officers that I was able to take valuable information from. But at least for me, there was one that I despised. She really made an impression on me and the things I learned from her were not law enforcement related. They were the characteristics that I did not want to be. Ironically, she was the first officer that I remember speaking in depth to me about an officer at another department creating havoc among the ranks. At that point I wasn't very interested. However what I learned later would prove to put me closer to the events than I would ever imagine.

While I was a cop, I was also the Assistant Security Manager for Kaiser Permanente hospital. This is where I would learn more about this horrible officer that broke the meaning of police brotherhood. I heard of an investigation at the El Cajon Police Department. It involved one of my security officers at the hospital. He was later arrested off duty for actions involved in the investigation. I must remind you, from this point forward, this is all hearsay and I was not a part of the investigation in any manner.

Security Officer "B" was terminated from his employment and an on-going investigation was being conducted. I recall "B" hanging around the security office quite often speaking about the investigation and how it was not fair. At that point I became interested in the matter and began to ask "B" questions about the investigation. The investigation, from what I understood, was regarding an officer and an explorer cadet that had sexual encounters with under aged females. The alleged attacks took place at or around a karate studio and someone's apartment.

"B" didn't hold back. He was sharing so much with me. After all, he was a pretty good employee, very popular among the other security officers, and I understood that his mother was a lieutenant at the El Cajon Police Department. He also had aspirations of becoming a police officer.

"B" always would speak about the case. Of course he told everyone that he was innocent and didn't have anything to do with the criminal acts. As I listened to him talk more and more, he told me the cop being investigated with him was Officer Kennedy. My thoughts then all clicked together and I asked if the cop had a wife that worked at Chula Vista PD. He told me he did. So now I was extremely interested in the case. I knew the wife of Officer Kennedy. She was a Chula Vista officer and I thought she was nice.

He kept me informed every step of the way, through the investigation, court process and eventually the penalty phase. I remember asking "B" several times about the beginning of the investigation. How did it all come about? He told me that there was this El Cajon cop, LaChapelle, and that he had it out for Kennedy. That part I didn't understand. He told me that LaChapelle didn't get along with anyone on the department, was a "religious freak" and was a real "a—hole". I remember "B" telling me that the cop that started this was a "jerk" and someone that should never have been a cop. "B" had a severe problem with the way this case was being handled.

Over time I thought about the case, the people involved and the officer that brought it all to the forefront. It was hard for me to believe that there was a cop out there that committed horrifying criminal sex acts. Worse yet, there was an employee of mine that was involved in the criminal acts as well. To top it all off, I now had mixed feelings about the cop that started all of this. What was he thinking? How did it affect his career? What was his future going to be like? Would I really want to be friends with someone like that? I would have all of my questions answered years later!

Almost a decade later, I met Officer K. M. LaChapelle. Only thing, he is no longer a cop. We ended up working together on several details. I introduced myself to him and sat in his office for a couple hours. During that time we swapped typical cop war stories and that is when I found out that he was the "cop" that completed the infamous internal investigation that I was already somewhat familiar with. What a small world. We spoke about that for quite a bit of time and I was just amazed. This guy seemed pretty cool and he was not the guy I was led to believe took down an entire department.

It has now been a couple of years, and Kevin and I are extremely close. Our work ethic is very similar, our beliefs are comparable, and well, I like this guy. He and I both studied Organizational Leadership and practice those theories learned in our own departments. We frequently meet for lunch, coffee, or just to hang out in the office and talk about the world today. While you are reading this book, place yourself in my position and see how the events come full circle. I knew of this person and was made to believe that this person can't be trusted and was someone that I would not like. That is quite far from the truth. I consider Kevin a close and personal friend. I trust him with my life and learn from him each time I see him.

Now he has written this book using his own experiences, thoughts, and techniques. I trust that by reading this book you will have a deeper understanding and appreciation into the psyche of one man and his fight for justice.

David LaChapelle, Former Police Officer, City of La Mesa, California

Kevin has always been a very passionate and goal orientated individual. Kevin has had a very clear vision of right and wrong and where he stood on that issue, which was the right side.

This began in childhood from refusing to join others in childhood pranks that he knew were illegal to making his objections known if he believed that friends or family were headed down the wrong path.

Kevin's dream was to become a police officer. As we grew up in Denver and played cops and robbers Kevin would refuse to play with us unless he could be the cop. We always agreed because we got such a kick out of watching the tenacity he would take in his role-playing.

After being honorably discharged from the U.S. Navy myself, I too became interested in law enforcement and immediately applied and was accepted into the police academy. I was glad that I was able to guide Kevin towards his law enforcement dream and remember vividly the pride on his face when he graduated from the police academy and proudly wore his El Cajon Police uniform.

Kevin quickly stepped up to his new position and immediately became a leader in his patrol function. Kevin also realized that his belief system and position of expected integrity was in direct conflict with some of his superiors on the department. Kevin refused to waiver and though put in some very disparaging positions, remained steadfast in representing his badge with honesty and integrity.

Kevin was instrumental in working with the community, especially troubled youth. This brought much applause from the community but much resentment from some within the El Cajon Police Department. This was a new guy who was receiving numerous accolades for a job well done with the community while at the same time the rest of the department had much conflict with the community.

At the time, I was a police officer in the neighboring city of La Mesa. Kevin realized that he was in conflict with some of his superiors and was very careful not to belittle his department or pull me into the conflict. I was very fortunate to be in on a police department that was of the utmost of integrity and had a reputation of such. This was in contrast of the reputation that the El Cajon Police Department had. I felt bad for Kevin being in the situation that he was in, but at the same time, knowing that if anyone could show or bring about change for the better, it was Kevin.

There were a few times that Kevin phoned me and told me that he was in fear for his life and gave me directions of who to talk to and where records were kept in case something happened. I was sad when he left law enforcement because I truly believe that it was his calling.

If Kevin had been on any other police department in San Diego County, I believe the outcome would have been completely different and he would still be a police officer protecting the community and living his dream.

Though I have not always agreed with Kevin, I have never questioned his integrity, honesty or desire to do what was right under any situation.

CHAPTER ONE

I Want to be the Good Guy

Graduation Day—the day I'd been waiting for since I was a kid! I was about to be commissioned as a police officer after completing the police academy. I looked around me and saw many of my classmates with whom I'd spent the last 12 months completing a training academy that had stretched all of us to our limits, both physically and academically. Waiting for my name to be called so I could go forward to receive my commission, I wondered how many members of my class would stay with the job over the next few years. Some were as dedicated as I was, but I knew others were there for different reasons—a good job, protected civil service benefits, and a chance to be in uniform, complete with a macho image of being a tough cop.

My dream had always been different. I viewed a police officer as a servant of the community, someone to whom people in trouble could turn to in a crisis, someone who could make a difference in the world around him. I could not know then how much my beliefs would be tested in the years ahead. But on that incredible day, I was excited, and eager to fulfill my dream of being a police officer. I already had a job waiting for me in the City of El Cajon, California, and I was on my way at last, ending one journey that began when I was a kid and beginning a new one, where playing "cops and robbers" would soon be replaced with a real career as a police officer.

Cops and Robbers

All boys play games that let them pretend to be heroes. It's a way of testing their ability to win, to overcome obstacles, and to believe that the good guys always win. For my father's generation, the game was probably cowboys and Indians, but for me and my friends, the game we played the most was cops and robbers from the time we were about seven or eight years old.

Our view of good vs. evil was pretty simple back then, fueled by television shows where the tough but fair police detective always solved the crime and put away the bad guys at the end. And just like

1

on TV, the good guys, the cops, always won in our games. Although we were supposed to take turns, I always insisted on playing the cop. To me, right winning over wrong was the only way to go, and I decided then that I wanted to be a police officer when I grew up. Maybe it was because my dad was a fireman, and I grew up in a home where public service was highly valued, but I think the big influence that solidified my goal was meeting Ray Ruybal, a police officer for the City of Denver, Colorado, when I was fourteen. He would give me a ride home whenever he saw me walking home from work. I admired his strength of character and the way he handled himself with the confidence that he was protecting the community. He became a role model for me and helped me see the police not as tough cops but rather as people who were there to keep the peace. And to me, a police officer has always been just that—a *peace* officer.

God Has a Plan

I grew up in a religious Catholic household, even attending a private Catholic school from kindergarten to the ninth grade. After searching for God on my own, I discovered that I could have a personal relationship with Him outside of any religious structure. I always was a bit of a rebel and had quite a short attention span. For example, during Mass while serving as an altar boy, I would intentionally ring the bells at the wrong time and then look out at my Mom to see if I had been able to get a rise out of her. Even while sitting in a pew, I would pick up and drop the kneelers at some of the quietest times during the service. I always had a difficult time having someone tell me how to get to God by their means. I always believed I could have a personal relationship with God. I have a very intimate relationship with Him in which I talk to God in prayer, even while just driving down the street.

I have never wavered in this one belief: God has a plan for each of us, and I knew He had a plan for me and would direct my life into a path where I could do the most good. Of course, I believed then, and I still do now, that I needed to be aware of the opportunities to find out what that plan was and how I could follow it. Even in my early teens, I was convinced that this plan included my becoming a police officer so that I could make a positive difference in the community where I would work. The only difference between then and now is that I thought then that being a police officer would be my life's work and only learned later that it was just a small part of God's plan for me in the years ahead.

God seemed to always send just the right person into my life at the right time to teach me valuable lessons. For example, an elderly neighbor couple had a huge impact on my early teenage years. Mr. and Mrs. Sylvester taught me so much in life. I would watch them at their best and worst. I recall times when I would sit for hours listening to their words of wisdom. I always admired how Mr. Sylvester would take care of his wife and tend to her needs. She had serious medical problems. Mr. Sylvester had a heart attack and needed a lot of attention himself. I was there for them whenever they needed help. I rigged a panic alarm that he could press in which it would page me on a beeper, alerting me that they needed help.

One time he bumped the button in the middle of the night. I can remember waking up to the sound of the alarm. My mom heard me getting up. "What happened," she asked. "Mr. Sylvester is calling for help!" I threw my clothes on and ran down the street to their house. I had keys to their house and stormed in to render aid. They were sound asleep. My storming in probably gave them a heart attack in itself. Mr. Sylvester awoke telling me that he must have rolled over on the button setting it off. He was happy that I responded as it gave him a secure feeling knowing I was there for them. I sure was glad it was a false alarm though. It did however wake me up to realize how serious this could be. The next week I went and took a CPR class to make sure I was equipped to help them in a medical emergency.

When I was about 16 years old, Mrs. Sylvester passed away. It was not long after that Mr. Sylvester had a heart attack and was hospitalized in critical condition. I went to the hospital to visit him. It was so hard. I tried to fight away the tears. He appeared so at peace. He told me not to worry. The paramedics had lost his heartbeat for several minutes while on the way to the hospital. He shared with me how he felt so close to the Lord. Often he and his wife would share scriptures from the Bible with me. He told me of a vision he had of his wife and that they were together in a garden and he could feel the presence of the Lord. He told me of how he knew he was nearing the end of his journey here on this earth. He was excited to go and be with the Lord and he comforted me. He seemed so anxious to leave here and go to heaven to be with God and his wife. He died the next day. When I heard the news, I can remember walking home from school and just crying so hard. I would miss him very much.

God also had sent my Mom's best friends Frank and Janis Osweiler to help guide me. I was a difficult kid to deal with. Not many people had patience with me other than my Mom, even though she did not think she had patience, she did. I still don't know how she put up with me as a kid. Frank and Aunt Janis (as I called her) were the ones to set me straight. They always made sure I knew they were watching and did not approve of my behavior and especially how I treated my Mom. Till this day we still keep in touch. I always appreciated the older people God would place in my life to give me wisdom and guidance.

There was my Mom who has always been the most influential person in my life. She has passed on so much to me. Her consistency in helping others has always had a profound impact on my life. She always has and still continues to make incredible sacrifices for others, including taking in her family rather then sending them to nursing homes. Then my Dad taught about fixing things. He passed on to me a lot of skills. He could build or fix anything. What I lacked from him, God seemed to provide for me through others. I had always wished for a dad who would talk to me about life and give me advice. I wanted a dad who would hug me and tell me everything would be okay. I later found that what I always sought after from my dad is what I would be for the many individuals whom I would mentor. I would be for them the very thing I had wished for while I was growing up.

Then there was my oldest brother David. He would take me in when I was almost 20. In 1986, I moved from Denver, Colorado to San Diego, California. I was in a rut, and my life seemed to be spinning in circles. He was not into taking much crap off of me as well. He knew my games and was not about to play them. It was living with him and his wife that helped me gain some solid footing in life and begin to grow. Being away from my Mom made me realize how horrible I was. I recall making a video and sending it to her telling her how sorry I was for being the rotten kid I was. Now I was ready to find the will of God for my life.

David was a San Diego Sheriff's Deputy at the time. He later joined the La Mesa Police Department which was a neighboring city to El Cajon, where I would begin a police career. David and I still have a very strong bond. We had been through a lot together and consistently stood by one another.

I wanted so badly to know what God's plan was for me. I knew I wanted law enforcement, but was

that God's plan too? I would hear people say they could hear His voice, yet, I had never heard it. I would lie down in bed at night and ask God to appear in my room. I would say, "God, if you are real, please come appear right here in my room." I would try to wait up for Him, but then would fall asleep.

One time while walking along the boardwalk at Mission Beach, my attention was drawn to a man standing by the sea wall facing the ocean. His back was to me; however I could sense he was probably homeless or down and out. I did not know why I felt drawn to him. I looked at the back of him and thought, "God, why am I drawn to this guy, am I suppose to talk to him?" I finally walked over to him. Not knowing what to say, as I opened my mouth, the words just seem to flow. I said, "Hey bro, God loves you and has a plan for your life!" He turned to me, and I could see he was crying. He then began to cry harder. He told me that he had been contemplating suicide, and had asked God if He was real to make Himself known to him. This was just immediately prior to my coming up to him. This was the first time I recognized how God could draw me to someone. All of my life I would hear people say that God had spoken to them, and I thought they were hearing an audible voice. Now I realized what it meant to be sensitive to God's voice. I never forgot that indescribable feeling of knowing that God was nudging me to tell someone something.

Getting Started

There was just one little problem with realizing my goal: to enter the Police Academy, a candidate must be at least age 21, so I had some time to fill before I could begin. School had always been a struggle for me because I was said to have ADHD—attention deficit hyperactive disorder, which affects somewhere between 3 to 7% of children in this country. Only in my adult years would I recognize some of the difficulty I still face because of this problem. For me, ADHD in boyhood manifested itself in my having boundless energy but a difficult time concentrating in school. As a result, my reading skills were poor, and my academic performance was always weak. I knew the Academy would pose a tough challenge, but I was determined that somehow, someway, I would master the demands of the course.

Because I had a few years to fill after high school while I waited for that all-important twenty-first birthday, I had several short-term jobs after high school, working at fast food restaurants, a 7-11 store, and finally at Home Depot, where I gained confidence in my abilities. I started as a cart attendant, then became a cashier, next worked in receiving, and finally was promoted to a loss prevention manager where I was able to significantly reduce employee injuries resulting in a major reduction in workers compensation claims. I found I had a real talent for the work and even considered staying with it for a time. Then I saw an ad for a

Police Academy regional training program in Southern California, where candidates could apply for entry. I signed up along with a couple of other friends, all of whom were excited about their new careers.

The three of us who knew one another were all in the same class at the Academy, and we settled in for a long series of classes on legal issues, elements of crime, arrest procedures, firearms training, investigative procedures, and intensive  physical training. Of the three, I had always been the weakest student in school and hated the physical fitness regimen which required running several miles. Of course, I found a way to compensate for my weakness. I would run alongside the weakest students, encouraging them to keep going—when, in fact, I could barely keep up with them. By encouraging the others, I found it helped me to get through it because if I was telling them they could do it, it forced me to be able to do it as well. My performance at the Academy was so good that I was offered a job even before I graduated.

Not everyone made it past the Academy, and I remember one friend Steve, who like a lot of our fellow students, tended to party hard. On his 21st birthday, Steve was returning home from an evening out on the town and was pulled over and got a "DUI"—driving under the influence—arrest that ended his police career before it even began. Many times before I had discussed with him the danger his drinking posed to his future, but he just would not give it up, and it cost him his career.

There were probably a lot of others at the academy who didn't get caught but who could have just as easily ended up in the same predicament. I remember thinking that these guys are drinking and driving and they will be pulling over other motorists for the very same thing—and probably arresting them. I knew that to be successful, I would have to lead by example and become a role model to others in the community.

As one of the survivors on graduation day, I was looking forward to starting my new job right away. On that day, the word "rookie" had a nice ring to it, and I could hardly wait for my first day on the job.

Chapter Two

Rookie Time

My first day on the job—October 4, 1989. I remember it so clearly that it seems like only yesterday. Although I had not fully completed my Academy training, I was allowed to begin the first of three phases of my training with the City of El Cajon, California, Police Department prior to graduation so I could get a head start and be ready to go on patrol as soon as I graduated. The first order of business was being sworn in by Chief of Police, Jack Smith.

For me, taking the oath as a police officer was as solemn a vow as any I had ever made. The words "to protect and to serve" echoed in my mind long after the brief ceremony and handshake from Chief Smith. I felt that I would spend the rest of  my life doing just that as part of a police force committed to the community's welfare. At last, I believed I was fulfilling God's plan for my life.

My first training officer gave me experiences I will never forget—and one I could hardly believe. There I was, so new that my uniforms weren't even ready yet, riding around in a patrol car, with passersby turning to look at us as we cruised past. It was a dream come true, and I said a silent prayer that I would be worthy of the trust placed in me to protect and serve the community.

I knew God had called me to perhaps the most powerful profession possible where every day I might make a difference in someone's life. I knew I could be such a strong light for justice and compassion for others. Daily I would pray and ask God to lead me in the right direction. I wanted to be in the right place at the right time. I knew God would be with me always and deeply involved in my work. While I rode with other officers, I knew that God was my real partner!

Even in my excitement and enthusiasm, I felt a cold shock of reality during my first training assignment. My training officer was a bit like a parent who sets a bad example for his children. I was filled with this sense of excitement that we were really working to care for the community, but my training officer was of a different mind. Maybe he had become jaded over the years, seen too much of the bad side of human nature, but the effect on me was chilling. On more than one occasion, I watched him spot someone walking toward our car to ask for assistance, and he would pretend not to notice, roll up the window, and just drive off. His goal seemed to be to do only the minimum required

on the job. He seemed to run more personal errands and "hang out" at his house rather than handle police calls. I knew that to complain would only have ended my career early, so I silently resolved never to let myself become like this officer.

My next training officer was different. He spent time talking to the people in the neighborhoods we patrolled and tried to be make a difference.

An Un-Typical Day

Perhaps I should start by saying that there is no typical day in police work. Sure, there is a lot of routine—including paperwork for every arrest or incident—but no two days were alike. The most common calls were for domestic violence, usually a husband who was drinking or using drugs who would take out his anger on his spouse. Sometimes, a husband and wife would both be arguing and fighting, so it was difficult to discern just who was at fault.

If I did have to arrest someone at their home for domestic violence or on a warrant for another offense, I would suggest that the children be sent to the other room first so they wouldn't have to see a parent being handcuffed and taken away and the parent wouldn't have to be embarrassed in front of their kids—something I learned from my second training officer. One time I had to arrest TJ Delgado's father for domestic violence. TJ was 14 at the time. I talked to him afterwards and explained that his dad needed to get some help so he would be a better dad. From that time on, every time I would drive down TJ's street, he would wave to me. That connection gave me the feeling that I was doing right in God's eyes.

I also learned very quickly what not to say during a call of domestic violence. During one such call, I saw that the wife appeared to be pregnant. I commented to the husband how horrible it was for him to hit his wife especially when she was pregnant. Unfortunately, she was not pregnant. She snapped back at me, "I'm not pregnant!" Oops, I quickly recovered.

One thing that always struck me when responding to calls of domestic violence. It seemed to always be the same old story. Boyfriend and girlfriend living together, boyfriend lost his job, and they just sit and fight all day long. I would often notice that there would be very little food for the kids, but they always seemed to have enough money for a case of beer in the refrigerator and a carton of cigarettes on the counter. It did not take long to figure out that the kids were not a priority for many of these people. Seeing this over and over again would sicken me.

Still I went through a time when I found myself being heavy-handed, and all the other officers seemed to love it—at last I seemed to be like them, but I soon got over that attitude and was ashamed of it afterwards. It was difficult because here I was trying to do what is right, yet I would go to calls when people would come against me because of the uniform, and at times, I would just say, "Hold on, we are the police, and you are going to jail and I am not going to get hurt taking you in—*you* are!

Some of the things you go through while being a police officer begin to shape you. A few calls that had lasting impact on me happened shortly after I had completed my training.

One very profound call occurred when I was driving down Marshall Street in El Cajon when a call came out of shots being fired at the Main Street Trolley Station. I was almost right there. I advised dispatch that I was coming up on the scene. As I arrived, I could hear no gun shots. I asked dispatch to confirm shots were being fired at the Trolley Station to which they confirmed that there were reports of shots being fired. I parked my police car on the sidewalk, got out and began strategically moving toward the main area of the station. I then heard a gun shot and saw a female with a gun chasing a male and firing at him. The male was running in between cars trying to dodge the bullets. Finally, I came upon the female. I was sighting her in with my firearm and was ready to shoot her if she did not drop the weapon. While I was preparing to take her down, she pointed the gun into her mouth and pulled the trigger. I was shocked as I had never seen a human being pull the trigger on themselves and fall to the ground. It reminded me of a time I worked on a ranch and a horse had broken its leg and had to be put down. They shot the horse in the head with a rifle, and I will never forget seeing the horse just drop to the ground so lifeless. It was a familiar feeling seeing the girl fall to the ground, and she was dead. She had confronted her boyfriend after learning that he had been cheating on her. Unfortunately, she decided to bring a gun with her.

I remember another time when I received a call of shots fired in an apartment complex. Upon arrival, it was like a movie. As I exited my vehicle looking for cover, I heard shots. As I neared the complex, I found one person lying in a pool of blood. Upon rounding a corner, I came face to face with a man in his fifties yelling, "Who wants it next?" I finally took aim at him, and was tightening my finger on the trigger of my firearm, ready to fire shots to his chest and head. He was pointing the gun off in another direction, and when I yelled at him, "Police, drop the weapon," he turned his head to look at me, but maintained his gun pointing in another direction. I was waiting for him to point the gun in my direction, and I was going to take him out. He threw the gun down to the ground, and was taken into custody without incident. He had come over to his daughter's house because her boyfriend had been abusing her. When her dad confronted the boyfriend and his friend, a dispute ensued, and the father took out his gun he had brought with him, and fired at them.

One minute you are just on routine patrol and the next minute you are in a knock down drag out fight. During one holiday season, either Thanksgiving or Christmas, I cannot remember which one, I responded to provide cover to another officer. Upon arrival, I saw that he had two biker type individuals sitting on the curb. After I arrived, the officer told me he wanted to search both subjects to make sure they did not have any weapons. As soon as the first subject was told to stand up to be searched, the fight was on. This guy put on a fight like never before. He obviously had something to hide, but what was it? We struggled to get control of him as he seemed to have never ending strength. He was under the influence of drugs. At one point he was pulling away from us trying to get back to his car. This was not going to happen, as we knew the potential of him getting a weapon from his vehicle. At one point he even tried to grab for the other officers handgun. I finally took out my nunchukas and began striking this subject as hard as I could in the arms. Nothing fazed him. At one point, as I was swinging the nunchukas, he was able to pull the other officer back into the mix and positioned the other officer between myself and him. As I swung the nunchukas, it struck the other officer in the head. Now I had swung the nunchukas as hard as I possibly could, and the officer went down and was bleeding profusely from his head. Now it was just me and this guy fighting. We rolled down an embankment while we were struggling. I had already called for more officers, but the wait for them to arrive seemed to be hours. Finally the additional officers arrived and we were able to get this guy into custody. Boy did I feel bad about striking the other officer in the head. I would never live this one down. After this incident, whenever I would pull out my nunchukas, everyone would get out of the way!

While stopped at a light on Fletcher Parkway and Cuyamaca in El Cajon one sunny afternoon, I noticed an older male on a bicycle next to the curb waiting for the light to change. All of a sudden, I saw him just fall over to the ground. I jumped out. This guy was in full cardiac arrest! He was not breathing and had no pulse! I called for paramedics on the radio and then began CPR. This was only the second time I had performed CPR. The first time was on an elderly male who had emphysema, and he died. This time, it seemed to go a little easier because he was already on the ground whereas the elderly man was in a recliner chair and I had to get him to the ground by myself. While I was performing CPR, a man pulled over and identified himself as a Trauma E.R. Doctor. He even had a medical bag with him. This guy was a pro. He was so calm and confident. He told me I was doing well with the CPR and to continue while he set up some equipment. He began inserting a device down the throat to maintain an open airway. The paramedics arrived a short time later and began shocking the man to try and get his heart going again. I asked the doctor if he thought the guy would pull through, and he said it was 50/50. I figured the guy probably died, but a few weeks later, the man came into the police station to pick up his bike that I had impounded. He also wanted to thank me for saving his life. It was so odd seeing this man walking and talking because the last time I had seen him, he was dying, and frankly did not look like he would make it.

There was another life and death situation that comes to mind. During the rainy season, many young people will play in the drainage ditches throughout the city. The problem with this is the fact that the current actually is stronger than one may think. Once you get sucked into the current, it is not easy to break away from it. If you get to certain areas, the water is driven below ground. If a person is sucked into those drains they will have to endure a half mile of traveling underground and often underwater until the drain goes above ground again. Typically, if someone were sucked into this, they would drown. One day, two 14 year old boys decided to play in these drainage ditches. They were sucked in and could not get out. As they were being swept away, officers were trying to get ahead of them, and then try for a rescue. I was near the area in which the water travels underground. If the kids got passed me...Well...That was it for them. I figured that officers further east from me would be able to grab the kids. I listened on the radio as I heard officer after officer saying that they were not able to rescue the kids. The kids were still heading west and almost near where I was. I knew if I did not grab them, they were probably not going to survive. I was looking for anything I could such as rope, but only found jumper cables. I took my police gun belt off and positioned myself to grab the kids. As they were heading my way, I saw a fire truck arriving near where I was. As the kids neared me, I was yelling at them to kick their feet to position themselves closer to me. I stretched out my hand as far as it could go, and held out my baton yelling for them to grab it. I was able to at least hold them into position, but could not get the leverage to pull them out. I yelled up at the firefighters to throw me their red line fire hose. As they threw it to me, I was able to get the kids to grab it and we pulled them to safety. It felt good to get them out. It was quite an effort for a lot of officers. The kids were pretty scared and shaken up. I later received the Police Star Award for rescuing them.

Pranksters at Heart

Another Officer I would soon meet would be a partner in our efforts to reach the troubled youth of the community. Joe Sirard was hired at about the same time as I was. When we first met, we had no idea of how God would bring us together to help others. Joe, his wife Vicki, and their daughter Ashley, would become best of friends with me and my girl. Joe had a heart of gold. As soon as he saw that there was a need, he jumped on it immediately. I recall when a fellow officer was killed in a car accident; Joe stepped in immediately to provide a fundraiser to help the family of the fallen officer.

I enjoyed playing tricks on Joe as well. We were pranksters and knew no limit. I can remember one time when we saw one of the sergeants at a local Denny's restaurant. The police cars were keyed alike, so our keys fit the sergeant's police car. We pulled up, open the sergeant's passenger door and began engineering our prank. We tied a piece of string to the switch that activated the lights and siren. We wrapped it around the shotgun and then tied it to the driver side door. We then parked across the street to watch. The sergeant walks out of the restaurant and puts his keys in to unlock his car. As he opens the car door, the lights and siren blared and he frantically tried to get in and turn off the sirens as quick as possible. He was mad! He called me on the radio, because like when I was a kid, everyone usually knew it was me, and requested I meet him. When I did, he was mad, but had that little smirk on his face. He knew it was the best prank ever, and he had to love us for it.

On another occasion, Joe distracted a different sergeant enough for me to steal a cigar out of his jacket pocket. I then used the pin on the back of my badge to put a pinhole in the packaging. I then insert the little cigarette loads that you can buy at a magic store. This was a full size cigar, so I figured I needed a little more firepower. I inserted a couple more into it. I walked back in the watch commander's office, and slipped the cigar back into his jacket pocket. Later the sergeant lit up his cigar and got the shock of his life. It exploded with the end of the cigar looking like something out of a cartoon. However, the sergeant thought it was a defect of some sort with the cigar. Are you kidding, we wanted the credit for this one. So, we confessed during the next days shift meeting.

While on patrol, I would love to see Joe laughing as hard as he could. One time we were driving through a little strip mall. There were transients in the area. I saw a little dog walking across the parking lot. I pulled up behind the dog, and turned on the public address speaker. I yelled at the dog, "Dog, stop and put your paws up!" I repeated this several times, until I finally got bored. The transients thought we were serious and watched with amazement.

Sometimes I would use my sense of humor to lighten things up. After arresting a man for drunk driving, I had to transport him to the hospital to draw blood. Upon arriving at the hospital, I noticed the nurse drawing the blood seemed to be having a bad day. While she was completing her paperwork, I was completing my arrest report. When I came to the physical description of the suspect, I asked him, "How much do you weigh?" "How tall are you?" He responded by saying he did not know how tall he was. I glanced over and could see a giraffe measuring device affixed to the wall to see how tall kids were. This giraffe only went to five feet. I told the suspect to stand over by the giraffe so I could see how tall he was. I further told him that the giraffe only went to five feet, so he would have to duck. Because he was intoxicated, of course he did exactly what I had asked. He walked over to the wall, leaned up against the giraffe and squatted down. I looked at him and said, "Looks like you are about five feet." The nurse was on the floor laughing. It brightened her day, and that was just what I wanted to do.

After stopping a group of transients with a dog, I asked them for their names so I could run a records check to make sure they did not have warrants. After obtaining all of their information, I looked toward the dog, and asked the person holding its leash what the dogs name was. The person kind of laughed, but I remained very serious and without a smile. They told me their dog's name. I then asked what the dog's last name was. They again, looked confused and told me he did not have a last name. I asked if the dog was owned by them. When they said yes, I told them, "Well then the dog must use your last name. I then asked what the dog's date of birth was, how much the dog weighed, and how tall the dog was. The man looked at me confused and asked, "On all four or standing up?" I told him, "Does your dog normally walk around on two legs?" He then said, "Oh, well, I guess he is 15 inches tall. I then pretended to run the dogs name for warrants. I later told the man that his dog had a warrant out for his arrest. The man and his friends were stunned. I gave them my business card and told them to take their dog into the courthouse and go to the Marshal's Office and advise them that I told you your dog had a doggie warrant. To my surprise the man did just that. I received a call the next day from a friend of mine who worked for the Marshal's Office. He told me that the guy had come in and presented my business card and they knew right away I had been playing a joke.

During another radio call, the joke was almost on me. I received a call of a grandmother who was allegedly possessed with demons according to the family. While driving to the call, I remember laughing to myself thinking, "Give me a break, possessed!" I did not buy it. Upon arrival, I met with Officer David Turner. Officer Turner was an exceptional person. He had a genuine faith in God and was a strong role model for other officers. As we approached the house, a little old lady was sitting on the porch with a large family Bible on her lap. As we saw her, I told Turner, "I will handle this one." Dave laughed and

watched me walk up to the lady. She was sitting in a rocking chair with a little bit of a smile on her face. I said, "Hello, I am Officer LaChapelle, what is your name?" "Maria," she said. I said, "I see you have a Bible there, I am a Christian too." As soon as I said that, her demeanor changed, and she began to have a wicked look on her face. Her voice changed dramatically, and in a rough voice she began murmuring words that I could not understand. She then began yelling. Her family told us she was possessed and that they could no longer handle her. This lady was probably in her 80's. We could not get her to calm down. We finally called an ambulance to transport her to the hospital. Unfortunately, we were not able to get her strapped down to the stretcher. She went crazy, so we had to call for additional officers. We were afraid of hurting her. You can only imagine the officers getting the call to assist us thinking, "These guys cannot handle an old lady?" She had superhuman strength. It was unreal. After we finally were able to get her loaded up into the ambulance, I recall Turner telling me that there was more than meets the eye in this world. He began to share with me the spiritual battles that lie in realms unseen by man. I was really taken back by the strength of this elderly woman. A couple of years later, Officer David Turner was killed in an automobile accident. When we were told to come to the station to hear the news, it was devastating. Turner had shared his faith in God with me and Officer Joe Sirard on many occasions. In fact, the week before his death, he was telling us that it was imperative that our lives be right with God. He went on to admonish us that one never knows when they will die, and so they had better be right with God. Upon hearing the news, Joe and I just stared at each other, both of us remembering his words. Boy did I shed tears for Dave. What a man he was!

Serious Times for Serious Situations

There were other times when the mere presence of a police officer was enough to calm the violence within a family. One such family I grew very attached to. In fact, I still keep in touch with them. The dad was often drunk and abusive with his wife and kids. Two of the sons were involved in our boxing program. Danny and Tony were incredible guys. Often I would receive a call from the guys asking me to come by their home. I did not know until years later that they would call me knowing that when I was at their home, the dad would stop being abusive to them and their mom.

Even today I can see the scars in their lives from the abuse of their dad. Danny had a career as a professional boxer while Tony has had his problems, but now is doing better than he ever has. Danny's relationship did not work out; however his girl, Gina soared like an eagle. Gina had a tragic childhood having had her parents die at a very young age. Gina went to college, graduated, and is now a probation officer in Houston, Texas. She is an incredible person. We still keep in touch as well.

I will never forget one incident in particular that traumatized Tony forever. In 1996, we were assisting with an outreach program in Tijuana, Mexico. Rarely would I stay the night in Tijuana. However, for this project, I would need to return early in the morning and chose not to have to commute, and stayed the night. We were in one of the roughest areas of Tijuana called Grupo Mexico.

In the middle of the night, I was awakened by the alarm sounding on my Bronco. As I stepped outside of where I was sleeping to investigate, I immediately saw one of our night watch guys defending himself from a knife attack from a person wearing a bandana over his face. I yelled at the person and ran over to help defend the attack. I then saw multiple suspects swarming our camp all wearing bandanas over their faces. Some of them were firing rounds from handguns toward our camp. They began robbing every one of their watches, wallets, money, and jewelry.

The girls from the group were in a separate structure which was crudely constructed. The door had no lock, but instead had a large rock placed behind it to hold it closed. I knew that bandits such as these were known not only to rob people in Mexico, but to rape the women as well. We were being held at gunpoint and were helpless to defend everyone. Tony, who was 15 at the time, looked to me and asked, "Do you think they will kill us?" For the first time in my life, I did think that this was it, and that they would shoot us when they were done robbing us. I told Tony, "They just might kill us, so pray to God and get your life right with Him." I remember seeing tears running down Tony's face. I felt so incredibly helpless. Never have I felt this. I prayed asking God to please make them leave. I tried to reason with the bandits, but they just became angrier. I remember the evilness I could see in the eyes of the attackers. They were brutal men.

Some of the bandits began walking over to where the girls were staying. They started pounding on the door trying to force their way into the room. I was praying, "God, please don't let them get in, as they will rape the women!" They were unable to gain access to the room. I was thinking that all of the girls must have been pressing against the door from inside to hold it shut.

It seemed like we had been seized for hours, yet in reality it was only for maybe 30 minutes. The bandits finally began to leave. I immediately ran over to where the girls were staying. I pushed on the door and it opened, however I could feel the resistance of the rock which had held it closed. The girls were all in their sleeping bags, and I could hear them crying. I asked them who had been holding the door closed when the bandits were trying to gain entry. They said no one was holding the door, but they were all just praying and crying while hiding in their sleeping bags. I still get chills thinking about how God must have had an angel holding that door shut. It was unreal.

Tony's wife recently told me that even to this day; Tony refuses to go to Tijuana due to his being so traumatized by this incident. I too was affected for some time. For me however, I was more angered knowing that the people of Mexico are victimized so frequently and unable to protect themselves from such attack. I have never forgotten the feeling I had during this ordeal. This was the scariest encounter I had ever endured.

The Tarnishing of the Badge

I can recall during and after my phase training, I was surprised at many things that went on that I knew were not right. I recall a time when another rookie officer who was female, was having an affair with the internal affairs lieutenant. On one occasion, the female officer had come to the station while under the influence of alcohol and was involved in a verbal dispute with the lieutenant with whom she was having the affair. As she left the police station, she struck a couple of vehicles in the back parking lot. She then drove to a local Denny's restaurant, called the station demanding to talk with the chief of police. She said if they did not allow her to speak with him, she would kill herself. I figured she had really done it now. A week went by and she was again back on routine patrol.

This same female officer was having relationships with several other officers. The lieutenant became jealous and began stalking her in the evening hours as well as following other officers he suspected were having an affair with her. Many officers voiced concern for their safety due to the potential of this becoming a very volatile situation. The lieutenant retired a short time later. I carried this in the back of my mind, hoping and praying that I would never fall into such behavior.

I remember when an officer was caught having sex with a prostitute while on duty. He was married and had children. How could he be drawn into such a vice? He was using his position to intimidate and coerce the prostitute into having sex with him in order to avoid being arrested or cited.

Another officer was found to be dealing in stolen money orders. This officer was a DARE Officer. This was in the newspaper and many young people were really let down by this "role model" falling into such activities.

All of this was in a relative short amount of time. What on earth was happening with these officers? How did they come to make these decisions? I prayed, please God, don't let my badge tarnish!

A Mission Revealed

I tried to remain focused and be committed to what I knew to be right. One call had lasting impact on me and what my calling was to be. I responded to a call of a stabbing at a local county probation school called Summit High School. Upon arrival, there were about 20 students embroiled in a fight. I was very assertive upon arriving, and ordered all students to sit on the floor until I could gain control of the situation. Many students were belligerent and non-compliant. At one point I pulled out my police nunchaku and ordered them to the floor. They could sense the intensity and seriousness of my tone. They complied. After taking one of the suspects into custody, and securing the scene, I left the school to transport the suspect to the police station.

I was later called by the school principal and asked to return to the Summit School to explain my actions to the students because they believed I was too aggressive. Quite a few of the students were active members of gangs and just one step away from winding up in a juvenile detention center. When I first entered the classroom, my attitude was more than a little defensive. I had come there to lecture them on why I did what I did. I explained to them the fact that I did not know them,

and there was one of me and many of them. We talked about the fact that a violent felony crime had just occurred, and why it was so imperative for me to gain immediate control of the situation for my safety and for theirs.

As I talked and looked at that group of hostile, belligerent faces staring back at me, I knew I would never get through to them with a lecture. Slowly, my guard came down, and the next thing I knew, I was sitting on a desk chatting informally with the gang members. I felt a strong connection with them, and our bond was immediately recognized by both me and the gang members. I began talking to them candidly about what I had seen on the streets. I told them that their lives were all about choices they were making now and what those choices would mean for them later on. I told them how the choices they made now would impact their little brothers and sisters in their families who looked up to their big brothers as role models, and how their lives could make a difference in the world if they learned to work together. Finally, I told them that whether they knew it or not, God had a plan for each of them—a plan to use the very gift that He had given to them. I told them that they need to find their gift, pursue it and make all their decisions with that gift in mind. Before the session was over, the room was so quiet that, quite literally, you could have heard a pin drop. Many of them wiped tears from their eyes.

Serving the Community

After that, the principal of the school called Chief Smith and asked if I could come back again, that I had made a powerful impact on the students there—and I did go back many times and got many of them involved in community projects that focused their energy on positive things. Out of this grew a new program— Bridge the Gap—working with schools and the com-

munity to restore today's youth to become an asset to the community instead of being alienated. Bridge the Gap focused on the crisis of gangs and other disaffected young people by restoring them to their community's one person at a time. And when you influence one person for good, others follow like ever widening ripples in a stream, until many lives are touched for good.

My rapport with the gang involved youth was astonishing. I can remember on one occasion I was handling a radio call at 200 S. Mollison. It was a routine crime report. While I was taking the report, I heard screaming from outside in the courtyard of the apartment complex. A large woman under the influence of drugs had a hammer and was trying to go after other people. I exited the apartment and entered into the courtyard to find this woman swinging a hammer at people who were trying to get away from her. I drew my firearm and ordered her to drop the hammer to which she refused. I re-holstered my weapon and drew my police nunchaku to engage the woman and attempt to strike the hammer out of her hand. While engaging her, many of her family members began to try to keep me from taking her into custody. I called for cover on my radio. Soon the Sheriff's helicopter was overhead circling me. I could hear the pilot on my police radio advising other officers that I was surrounded and needed cover now! I was so focused on the woman, I was unsure how, but could sense that her family members were being held back from me. I then heard the pilot describing the scene say on the radio, "The officer is

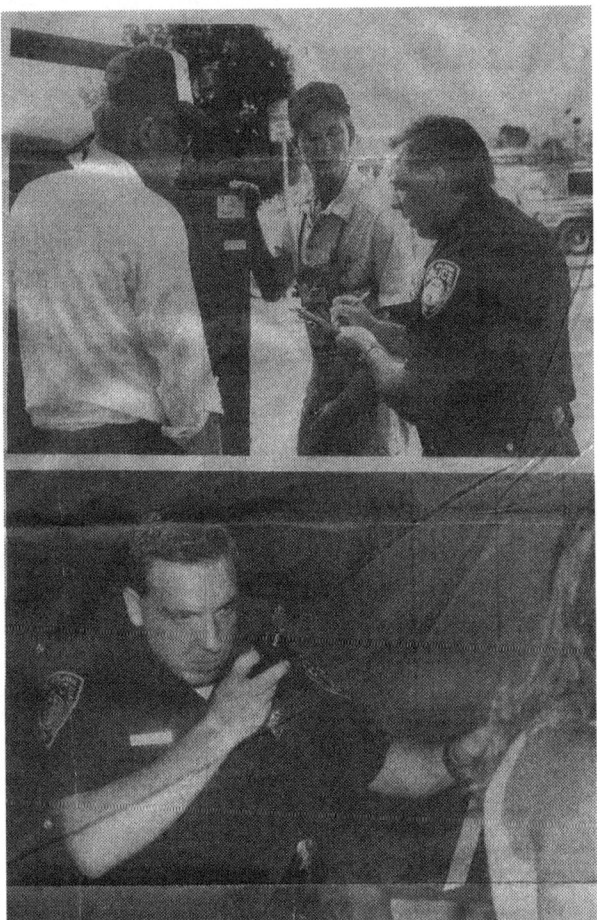

surrounded by what appears to be gang members, no wait, it looks like the gang members are actually helping the officer. Yes, the gang members are assisting the officer!" I looked over and saw several young people from the Summit School I had recently been visiting.

My relationship with the young people was rooted in my core values. I would begin to instill these values in their lives. I would preach a message of not only hope, but a message of accountability. I would teach them about decisions and being held accountable for their actions. It was not uncommon for me to receive calls from these young people confessing to crimes themselves, or telling me of crimes that their friends either committed or were about to commit. I can recall a case in which I arrested a sixteen year old for a strong-arm robbery. During my interviewing him, he confessed to a double homicide he and an associate had committed in Arizona.

His name was Travis Amaral. He began to tell me the story to which I had a gut feeling was the truth, no matter how far fetched it sounded. Often times I would hear confessions that were mere bragging alone. This was the real deal; I knew it from the beginning. This double homicide occurred on September 10, 1991. The victims, Bryan and Laura Bernstein had pulled over at a rest area off Interstate 8 just outside of Yuma. Greg Dickens and his 16-year-old accomplice, Travis Amaral, had been waiting near the rest area looking for the perfect victim to rob. Dickens told Amaral not to leave any witnesses. When they saw the Bernsteins get out of their car, Amaral walked across the interstate concealing a handgun that Dickens had previously stolen. They approached the Bernsteins, and Amaral pointed the gun at Bryan telling him to give Amaral his wallet. After Bryan gave Amaral the wallet, Amaral ordered the Bernsteins to walk past their car and toward the desert. Amaral then pointed the gun at pointblank range to the back of Laura's head and pulled the trigger. About 30 seconds later he shot Bryan in the back of the head as well. After hearing this story, and researching it, I found a case that matched exactly. Amaral was later extradited to Arizona where he and Dickens were convicted and are currently serving life sentences in Arizona.

This was just the beginning. God gave me this incredible opportunity in which people would open up to me and share things that would shock and stun most people. I knew I would use it to protect innocent people from people like Amaral and also to encourage gang members to begin to take responsibility for their actions.

I also was able to keep a lot of information in my head. I can recall another time when I was on my way to work. I turned on the portable police radio in which I carried and heard that the California Highway Patrol had been in a vehicle pursuit with a stolen vehicle and the suspects bailed out near Jamacha and Lexington. I just happened to recall a gang member Dallas Lopez who was into stealing cars. Dallas lived one block away at 225 S. Ivory. I called and advised units to check that residence. Low and behold, guess who answered the door dripping with sweat? Dallas Lopez, who admitted to being the driver of the stolen vehicle they had been pursuing.

On another occasion I met an individual who was a friend of another officer's brother. He began to share a story with me about his 18 year old brother who had disappeared. His brother's name was Jamie Peters. His VW bug was found abandoned on Mussey Grade Rd. and his body had never been found. I pulled the case from El Cajon and began to read through it and took an interest in trying to solve this homicide. There was a friend of Jamie's whose mother was a member of the Hell's Angel's. Her name was Maggie Diesen and her son Aaron was apparently beaten in the head with a bat shortly after Jamie's disappearance. The two were said to have been roommates. I made contact with Aaron whose mother was very reluctant to allow him to talk with me. He basically said Jamie was dead but would not tell me anything further. I began talking with many people who knew Jamie. I learned that before Jamie's disappearance, he had been working under the table for a family friend of the Peters named Jim Miller.

In addition, the mother of Jamie had hired a private investigator named Rick Post to look into her son's disappearance. I spoke with Rick on several occasions, and he told me he was convinced Jim Miller had knowledge and something to do with Jamie's disappearance. He felt that Jamie may have seen something he was not supposed to. According to Rick, Miller was into the distribution of methamphetamine.

Years later, in an unrelated case, Rick Post was kidnapped and taken to Mexico where he was tortured and killed. The suspects in that case were convicted. His murder had nothing to do with the Jamie Peters case. Post had been in a business dispute which police believe was the motive for the killing.

As time went on, no one wanted to talk about the Jamie Peters case. I tried talking to Jim Miller however he had nothing to say. Finally, the Peters family wanted to have a memorial service for their son and brother for some closure. They asked if I would speak at the service.

The crowd was maybe several hundred people, and while I was speaking, my attention was drawn directly to Jim Miller who was seated about five isles from the front. I began sharing the story of King David and Uriah from the Bible. King David had Uriah put to death to cover up his getting Uriah's wife Bathsheeba pregnant while Uriah was doing battle on behalf of King David. The analogy I used was that Uriah was betrayed by someone he trusted. I then looked directly at Jim Miller and said, "Like Uriah was betrayed by someone close to him, likewise, Jamie was betrayed by someone close to him. In fact, Jamie was killed at the hands of a close friend to the family, he knows it and I know it!" At that time, Jim Miller had his hands in his pockets, when I charged my assertion at him; he nervously jerked his hands out of his pockets, and in doing so, spilled his change all over the hard floor. While I was speaking, the room was incredibly silent, so when Jim spilled his change all over the floor, it was loud and drew the attention from everyone who all looked at him.

I will never forget that moment, the look of guilt written all over his face. The problem, we could not prove it. Many had since told me that Miller was using Jamie to distribute his methamphetamine. Either Jamie ripped him off or saw something, but they claim Miller had him killed and his body destroyed. The case has never been closed.

I had met a gangster named Eli Medina. This guy was very quiet. He had an evil streak that I always sensed with him. He was a little guy, and was always trying to prove himself. He dabbled into the gang scene, but nothing major as he was only 16 years old. His dad worked for the Department of Defense as a contractor and from time to time would be stationed abroad. One such time, he was stationed in Guam, and Eli would move there with the family.

He returned from Guam about a year later. Upon his return, he was involved in our program again. Something happened in Guam that really hardened his heart. He was different than before he left. Now, he was 17, almost 18, and he began getting arrested for things like auto theft. One time, I was interviewing him for a gang crime, and I began to ask him what had happened in Guam that had hardened his heart so much. He seemed like he wanted to tell me something but kept holding back. I continued to pull it out of him, and he finally confided in me that he had killed someone in Guam. I believe he said he had pushed someone down a cliff near the ocean. It was a place that couples would go to hang out called Lover's Point.

I contacted the Guam Police Department to inquire if there had been any homicides and described the area Eli said this had occurred. Nothing came up. I remembered the case of Travis Amaral in which he confessed to a double homicide, so I felt certain that Eli was telling me the truth. I was unable to go further.

Just this past year in 2005, I was sharing this very story with a criminal justice college class I was teaching. I had told them that over ten years ago a gang member had confessed to a murder in Guam. While I was sharing the story, a girl in the back of the room began to make distinct eye contact with me. I could see her becoming almost stunned. Her name was Charlotte. She raised her hand. I called on her and she began to share with me that she had just moved here from Guam, and that she worked as a clerk for the Guam Police Department. She told me that recently, a person was killed and when they recovered the body, they found a femur bone that was unrelated to the victim. She said it was in the same location that I described. I told her to see me after class. She did and put me in touch with

Detective John Perez who was assigned to the case. I submitted a letter detailing the story and gave him El's information. This was very recent, so I do not have the status of the case to date.

The Chief as my Mentor

Chief Smith was very supportive of these activities and knew that community outreach was desperately needed if a police force was to be able to meet the needs of citizens in the twenty-first century. Hired by then Mayor Joan Shoemaker, Police Chief Jack Smith had been brought in to restructure the El Cajon Police Department by introducing and implementing the concept of Problem/Community Oriented Policing through-  out the department. When he arrived in 1988 shortly before I was hired, Chief Smith received major resistance from the "old guard" police command he had inherited upon his arrival. Smith eventually left the department in 1994, after realizing that the change was not occurring, accepting a position with the San Diego Sheriff's Department. But that was still in the future, and we forged a close working relationship working together to cultivate and develop the police depart- ment's relationship within the community.

Chief Smith was originally from the Los Angeles Police Department. He told me on many occasions, "Kevin, you are a police officer before your time! Many people will resist the things you are saying and introducing into law enforcement. Don't give up, as you are a change agent. You have the vision and innovation that tomorrows policing must possess!"

In a short time, I was reporting directly to Chief Smith and engaging in other community outreach programs. Looking back, I can see how my closeness to the Chief engendered a lot of envy and resentment on the part of a few other officers who had been on the force for years, and I was definitely not part of the "good ol' boys' club". They resented a rookie's closeness to the Chief, and in particular, they resented Chief Smith and his attempts to transform the department.

Over the next several years, working with Chief Smith's encouragement, I excelled in my profession. I was designated Police Officer of the Year three years in a row! Ignoring the envy and lack of camaraderie from my fellow officers, I kept on going in the direction I was confident was right. I was a man with a mis- sion—to work with the people to build a better community. I really was thrilled with the work the Lord had laid out for me. I received decorations and awards for community leadership and accepted many engagements to speak on the role a police officer should have within the community.

My life was set, and I firmly believed that I was where God meant me to be, doing the work I loved. Life was good in spite of the resentment I felt from some fellow officers. I thought life would go on like that for me forever. But all of that was about to change. In fact, soon my life and career would face a major turning point, and one that I had never expected and certainly not one for the better.

CHAPTER THREE

Standing My Ground

As much as I was looking forward to my career, I learned early that not everyone had the same goal as I did—to protect and to serve the citizens around me. Once I arrested a known gang member for assault with a deadly weapon, and I knew that in doing so, I was protecting the neighborhood from violence. He was arrested on attempted murder, kidnapping, and other charges. I expected to be called to testify at a preliminary hearing, but after a long wait, I had heard nothing. Then I received an "Official Rejection Notice" from the District Attorney's Office, stating that the case would not be prosecuted. I was stunned and read the District Attorney's notice with disbelief. There in large black letters was the decision: "Defendants/witnesses/victims are all dirtbags." In another reject notice it read, "Victim is a dirtbag, no humans involved!"

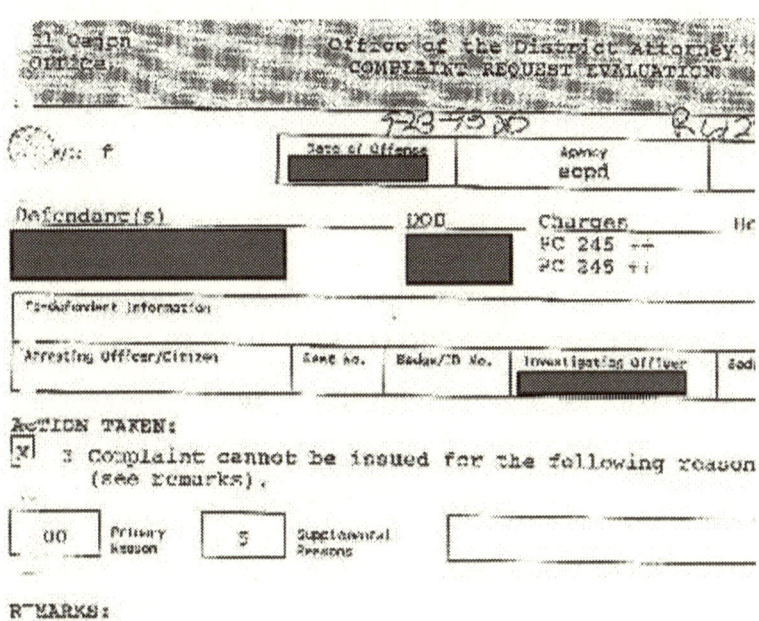

What could the District Attorney mean—"no humans involved"? The victim of the assault, a young Hispanic male, had no criminal record, and it was evident from the facts I had gleaned and from interviews with bystanders that the victim had been assaulted without provocation. Where was justice for the victim?

Unwilling to accept the decision, I went to the District Attorney's office and asked how this conclusion could have been reached. Here was a victim who suffered from an assault by a violent gang member. I also questioned the manner in which the reject notice was worded. My complaint was shrugged off. I was told that these gang attacks happen all the time—"Let 'em all kill each other. The point was that the victim was not a gang member. He was a school kid, with no gang ties whatsoever. They assured me that there were more "serious crimes" to handle.

As it turned out, there *was* a more serious crime to handle. Several weeks later, the same suspect, who had been released from jail, was involved in a standoff with a SWAT team. He was the suspect in yet another case involving kidnapping and murder. If he had been charged with the first crime, he would not have been on the street again. Now the District Attorney's Office finally had a "more serious crime" to handle. I was beginning to realize that there was both an undercurrent of racism and a disinterest in dealing with gang violence that permeated not only the El Cajon Police Department but all of San Diego County! The implication was that Hispanics must all be gang members—thus, because the victim was Hispanic, he must have been involved in a gang himself, and the District Attorney's Office was clearly not into seeking out justice as was their stated mission.

More Rejected Cases

That same year, the leader of a gang calling itself Orphans, was arrested for a double stabbing in El Cajon. The Orphans had been recognized as a major cause of violent crimes among the gangs in the city. This case, too, was rejected by the District Attorney's Office. The Deputy District Attorney's continued to reject serious cases involving gang violence by hardcore offenders because in their opinion, the victims were "dirt bags" and not worthy of having justice. Not long after the Orphans gang leader was released, he hit a kid in the head with a metal pipe. He had also committed many auto thefts, and was suspected in a carjacking. I would try and reason with the District Attorney explaining how crime would be reduced with even just this one gang member being incarcerated. I explained that many innocent victims of auto theft and maybe even carjacking could be spared if they would prosecute this criminal for the charges in which I had arrested him.

I even contacted the District Attorney's Special Operations Unit concerning these cases but was told nothing could be done. After approaching the elected District Attorney at the time, Ed Miller, for help, he advised me he couldn't help either as he was not going to be re-elected. While some public officials sympathized and may have privately shared my opinions, they feared taking on the powerful District Attorney's Office knowing they would suffer reprisals. Meanwhile, the problem continued to grow, and cases involving serious violence were being dismissed, based on the victim's reputation or race, or both. Meanwhile, serious hardcore violent gang offenders were being allowed to recruit young kids into their gang and perpetuate even more violence on the street.

Another incident occurred within the Juvenile District Attorney's Office and the San Diego County Probation Department. I had many friends on the probation department. A probation officer I will call "M" had a personal vendetta against fellow probation officer I will call "G". I knew of her dislike for him as she made it clear on many occasions. "M" and I were pretty good friends. I thought I knew her pretty well. We had worked many details together going after gang members. She knew of my reputation of having one of the highest felony arrest statistics within the police department. I knew that probation officer "G" had a son on probation. He had talked to me about his son and the fact that he wanted me to try and help his son change his life. I talked with his son on a number of occasions. I felt he could be helped. Unfortunately, I was never given that opportunity.

"G" had asked me if I would attend a court hearing to testify as an expert on gangs and if I felt I could help his son. I agreed to interview his son and see if I was confident in our program helping him. When "M" found out that "G" wanted me to help his son, she went ballistic. She tried many times to turn me against "G" which I pretty much just ignored her. When she realized I would not conspire with her little plan to sabotage "G's" son, she came against me with a vengeance. She and a District Attorney friend of hers tried to intimidate me into changing my testimony just minutes before the court hearing.

The District Attorney and "M" called me into an office and closed the door. They began to admonish me that the manner in which I testified today would determine the success or failure of my Bridge the Gap program. They then told me that they wanted me to testify to the judge that Probation Officer "G'"s son would not be accepted into my program. I was so incredibly insulted at their actions of coercing me to change my testimony for them. I told them of my outrage of their intimidation tactics and left their office heading for the courtroom. I then testified in court telling the judge of their pulling me into their office and attempting to intimidate me into testifying in a manner of their liking. To this day, I can recall the stunned look on the face of the judge. I do not know if the judge ever took any sanctions against them for their actions.

See Appendix A for a transcript of "G's" written complaint against "M" for her atrocious actions. To my knowledge "M" was disciplined for this incident, and we never spoke again. She used her position on a VIP program within the probation department to push me off of the board of directors in which I was a newly appointed member.

A Double Standard of Justice

I noticed that I seemed to be going against the grain. Swimming upstream which for many, seemed to be foolish. "You know what they say, you can't fight city hall," some would say. I was not willing to just give in to the status quo of the establishment. I was also learning that many of my fellow officers shared in my concerns; however they would tell me to keep up the good fight, but that they had families and could not risk their career.

Gradually, a sense of fellowship I might have felt at first in this "Blue Brotherhood" was being withdrawn, and I found that my views were scorned by others, especially those of the old guard—officers who had been on the force a long time and had adopted the attitude that minorities were entitled to less justice than those members of a white middle-or upper-class. We hear a lot of justice being affordable for those who were well off economically, but I was seeing this misguided principle in action. I actually saw officers drive away from what might look like a fight between minorities. They just couldn't be bothered. One time while I had a ride along in my patrol car, who was Latino, a Sergeant drove up and asked what I had arrested the guy for. He wasn't even in the back seat. The Sergeant asked me right in front of the ride along. The ride along, named George, told me it was okay, as he was used to this type of stereo typing from the police. He wanted to eventually become a police officer too. I told him how much he was needed to change this horrible behavior.

In the poor neighborhoods, in public housing projects, they were slow to respond to any report of a crime. I had been brought up to believe that everyone was entitled to a fair shake and to the full protection of the law when a crime was committed. Whether there was a report of a fight, domestic violence, or some other crime that didn't pose an immediate threat to an officer on the scene, I saw some of my fellow officers quick to view the victim as equally responsible as the perpetrator. The officers stuck together, ready to back each other's story up if excessive force was used in an arrest, and equally ready to ignore their responsibility for the safety of all the residents of poorer neighborhoods. I recall hearing things like, "That is what they get for living in this neighborhood!"

I faced repercussions from my persistence in trying to have violent crimes prosecuted, regardless of the victims' socioeconomic class. I was accused of "making waves," and was told to remain silent. I approached El Cajon Police Chief, Jack G. Smith, and told him what was happening. Chief Smith said he would take care of it, but did not—as I found later, he probably couldn't take care of it because he was facing a constant uphill battle to bring order and integrity to his own Department. Taking on the District Attorney was probably more than he could handle then. Although I never knew for sure, Chief Smith was probably warned to back off, even as I had been. Sometime later, under a new administration, the head of the East County District Attorney's Office was removed from office and things began to be cleaned up in the new District Attorney's Office.

Fitting In

Eventually, when anyone becomes surrounded by people whose attitude is less than honorable, what I saw and experienced and what I heard in the locker room and on the street began to have a negative effect on me. I was becoming steeped in a culture at work of aggressive action, use of excessive force, and an unwillingness to protect the community. I found myself gradually becoming part of that work culture, too.

Was it right? Of course not. Maybe I was subconsciously seeking acceptance instead of standing up to ridicule. When I got extra tough in making arrests, I was praised by the old guard. They thought I was coming around to their way of thinking. I began to actually get a kick out of showing a macho, aggressive attitude on the streets. At one level, I warmed to my new acceptance by my co-workers. But at another level, I was beginning to dislike myself.

Off the job, I'd think about all the ideals I had when I chose law enforcement as a career, and I didn't like what I was seeing in myself. I realized that I was becoming the very thing I disliked in the beginning, and gradually turned my attitude around again. While I was at peace with myself, I was moving toward war with my fellow officers. But I couldn't know then how deadly that change in my heart would be to my career. I would cry out, "Please God, don't let my badge tarnish!"

CHAPTER FOUR

An Officer and a Mentor

The more I saw of gang violence as a police officer, the more I realized that fighting crime among these young people with force wasn't working. When force was used, they became more rebellious, not less. I soon recognized that rules without relationships led to rebellion. I knew I would need to fight gang violence not with force, but with my heart. They needed mentors to encourage them to find a different path in life, one that would lead to purpose and productivity in their community. I began talking with them, one-on-one and in schools where I was invited to speak. I was invited into their homes to meet their families and began to get to know them not as gang members but as young men and women with tremendous unrealized potential and talent.

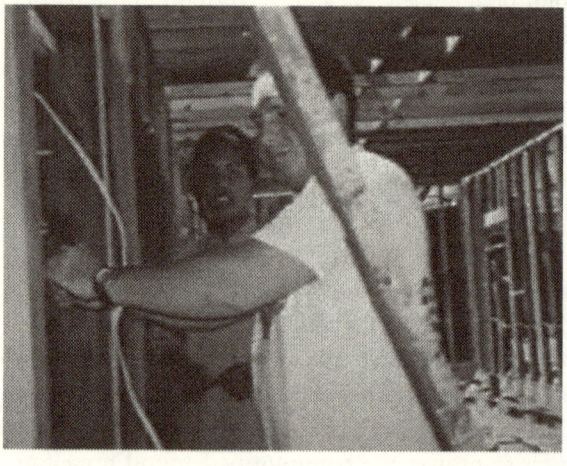

The Chief of Police encouraged me in my efforts of Mentorship to help the gang members in the community to make positive changes in their lives and to find alternatives to their current lifestyle. Many of these teenagers lacked a stable home environment, with one or both parents missing. Like all teens, they craved acceptance by their peers and were easily drawn into gangs where they were accepted, giving them a sense of self-worth as a member of a group. That road would inevitably lead to prison or death. Still, to many gang members, belonging to some group, however bad, was preferable to being an outsider with no strong relationships at school or at home. My goal was to help these troubled teens find a sense of self-esteem in a different way, to give them a new relationship that would point them in the right direction.

"He Takes Time for Us..."
—former gang member Ezequis Flores

I started the Bridge the Gap program, with Chief Smith's blessing, to help bridge the very real gap between these young people and the community, to give them a perspective that they were members of the community instead of being apart from it. The result was a mentoring program which gave the teenagers an opportunity to learn new skills, to develop new relationships, and to grow into productive adults. I can't say that every teen that entered the Bridge the Gap program was a solid success story, but most of them are now adults with families of their own, and some who have gone from being school drop-outs to getting college degrees.

I faced opposition from many who did everything in their power to undermine our program. I can remember a time that I sent a newsletter out at one of the continuation schools. My supervisor, forbid my sending this newsletter out. Her reason was that it sounded too religious. Teachers were stunned by this. You be the judge. Here is a verbatim transcript of the newsletter content in its entirety:

January 1993

The EI Cajon Police Department has started a six month School liaison pilot program. My name is Kevin LaChapelle, and I will be the School liaison Officer for the following schools: Chaparral High, EI Cajon High, Grossmont High, Cajon Valley Junior High, and Emerald Junior High.

The primary goal that has been set for this program is to have a safe environment for students, teachers, and the community.

I will be responsible for handling crimes that occur at the schools listed above, as well as providing positive direction for students. I will be there for students and teachers.

My main concern is that you become a productive member of the community. Some students are destroying themselves by using drugs and alcohol, joining gangs, and dropping out of school. I would like to see all of you make it in life. Success can be measured in many ways. For some it is money; for others it is happiness. Many times students do not realize that they are harming themselves. My job is to protect people. Sometimes that means to protect you from yourself. For instance, when students are involved in drug use, they do not always realize the problem. Until they stop using the drugs, and get better perspectives on their lives, they cannot help themselves. I ask all of you to trust me in helping you to succeed.

Many of you know me well, and know how much I care about all of you. I will never make a decision that will be harmful to you. Every time I make a decision, I will make sure that it is in your best interest. Sometimes people must be arrested showing that there are consequences for wrongful actions. Sometimes when I arrest someone, I am protecting that person from themselves. At other times I am protecting others from that person.

Take a look at your life and set goals for your future. Sometimes we hesitate to set goals for ourselves out of fear that we may not meet them. If you set goals and share them with others that care for you, they will want to help you. Some of you may be spinning in circles. Let me explain: Picture that you are out in the ocean in a life raft, drifting in circles. You cannot see any land, and are beginning to fear for your life. All of a sudden you catch a glimpse of a huge rock off in the distance. Now you have found hope, so you start paddling fast and hard to get to safety. You never take your eyes off of the rock, for fear of losing sight of it. Finally you reach the rock, and now you have a solid foundation in life. Find out what it is in life that you wish to seek. Do not take your eyes off of it, and do not let anyone sidetrack you, and you will reach your goal!

Some of you face troubled family lives. Others have few good friends. You must realize that you are not alone. I came from a troubled life. I can remember how dim the future seemed. Finally I was able to break away. I made a decision that I was going to meet my goals at all cost. I then began to plan a strategy to meet my goals. First I had to make sure that I did not allow anyone to interfere. I was not going to allow others to influence me negatively. I realized that my life could be affected by the people I hung around with. I began to associate with people who had good values. I talked to my friends and told them about my new goals. We then began helping each other reach our goals.

Now can be a turning point for us. I really hope that we can all make commitments to help each other. We are all in this together. Let us really love one another, and stop tearing each other down.

This is what I am all about. Life can be simple, yet we make it so complex. We cannot allow ourselves to continue along the path that we are following. Our world is being torn apart by drugs and gang violence. Too many students are harming their futures by dropping out of school.

Teachers and students, feel free to call on me. If I cannot help, I will find someone who can. Call me at 526.4300.

I am looking forward to working with all of you. Stand strong, and always do what is right!

DARE to Take a Stand

Being an example was the key in mentoring young people. I was sent to the LAPD's DARE (Drug Awareness Resistance Education) Academy. It was a very interesting experience. I met two other officers at this academy, one of which we still keep in touch. His name is Ramon Godoy. The first night, police officers from all over the United States and even some other Countries arrived for this training. The first thing I noticed was that the majority of officers were drinking alcohol excessively, and here we were at a DARE Academy where we would learn to teach the youth the dangers of alcohol and drugs.

Almost instantly, Ramon, Fabian, and I all seemed to catch each others eyes. I recall the three of us sitting separately, but looking around and watching what was happening at a mixer event designed to help us all get to know one another. After a short time, Ramon made his way over to me, and we introduced ourselves to each other. It was not long that Fabien joined us. The three of us immediately had a strong bond and we talked about our mutual interests in helping communities. We would all learn that all three of us had personal relationships with God.

Throughout the training, each night the same thing would happen over and over again. The officers would get drunk and act foolish. The next day they would sit in a classroom being lectured on the negatives associated with alcohol and drugs to which we must instill in our future students. This was so ironic.

For our final presentation, we had to give a lecture as if it were to young people on the dangers of alcohol and drugs. My presentation was much different than anyone might have guessed. Instead of speaking to the officers as if they were young people as we were instructed, I addressed the police officers as if they were my DARE Officer, and as if I were their student. I began the presentation by talking about how much of an impact my DARE Officer had on me and that I looked up to and respected him so much. I talked about the fact that he was the inspiration that I needed to resist alcohol and drugs and that I wanted to be somebody in life and be a role model just like my DARE Officer.

The closing of my presentation took a major turn. I told of a story right after graduating from the DARE program at my school. My parents wanted to treat me to dinner to congratulate me. We went to a local pizzeria. During dinner I am telling my parents how great my DARE Officer is, and how much I looked up to him. And then, I got excited because I saw that very DARE Officer eating dinner at the same pizzeria with his friends. I took my parents over to meet the Officer. As we approached, we could hear how boisterous he and his friends were, and I could see that my hero, my role model, was drinking the very alcohol that he said was dangerous for me. The look on his face was one that I would never forget. He did not say anything, for he knew the hypocrisy of his lessons at school that he could not follow himself.

You could hear a pin drop in this classroom full of police officers. The looks started off as sincere reflections of all of the partying these officers had done at night while learning about the dangers of alcohol and drugs in the day. That soon changed as they began to resent my calling attention to this, and then many of them shrugged it off as if to say, "Can you believe this guy, who does he think he is?" Some officers approached me later acknowledging that they needed to practice what they preached. I hoped they would remember that story. The bottom-line, if you are going to mentor someone, you had better practice what you preach or you will be more of a hindrance than anything.

Bridge the Gap

Starting Bridge the Gap took all my off-duty time and became completely absorbing as I began to see the changes these young people made in their lives; turning them away from violence and helping them see for the first time that there was a better life for them. I spoke in the schools, I organized boxing lessons, took the young people on ocean fishing trips—the first time away from El Cajon for many of them. We even went to Mexico to work on building projects for the poor, giving the young people who participated an understanding of how good it felt to do something kind for others. When these young people took their eyes off of themselves and their circumstances, and placed them upon others who were less fortunate, it had an incredible and lasting impact on them.

Business owners and leaders in the community began to support the program, seeing the beneficial effects of this approach to handling young people who had always been called "a problem." The program reinforced self-discipline and the participants began to gain a new vision of them-

selves and the possibilities that awaited them in the years ahead if they were to obtain a good education and learn new skills. For the first time, they were feeling a sense of self-worth, not from membership in a group but for the talent and skills they had to give to others. Instead of making the young gang members enemies as the Police Department had done in the past, we were making these teens allies in eliminating violence. The older hard core gang member of course had to be dealt with quickly and swiftly. My message to the older gang members; change your life and stop indoctrinating the young neighborhood kids into your gang, or face jail. They knew I was serious. I was known for gathering information on serious crimes, and pursuing the suspect and insuring they were brought to justice.

Inside the Department, Bridge the Gap was not met with cheers of enthusiasm from many of my fellow officers, who felt the only way to fight gangs was with force, but Chief Smith encouraged me to continue to mentor these young people because he saw the vision of what the community could be if at-risk youths could turn their lives around.

Program reaches out to youths

By Jo Moreland
Daily Californian staff writer

EL CAJON — Kevin LaChapelle is seeing his vision come true.

The El Cajon police officer's "Bridge The Gap" program for young people who are in or trying to avoid trouble opens the door of its own home Monday at 669 E. Main St.

It is the first time LaChapelle's nonprofit organization has had a place of its own, and it will be a uniquely youth-oriented site for East County.

"Blown away," the Bridge founder said in describing his reaction Saturday to finally having a permanent address.

"It's really motivated us all to just do that much more.

"We've been here all weekend setting it up. It's just awesome."

The young people are ready. An advance guard of about 60 kids showed up last Wednesday as refurbishing began, thinking the Bridge was open already.

Although parents are encouraged to get involved, LaChapelle doesn't need any more volunteers for Bridge staff right now.

He said about 40 people — parents, school personnel, people who work other child programs, business people, pro-

Please see PROGRAM, Page A2

Tim Cramer puts the finishing touches this week on a logo he helpes his father paint for Bridge The Gap's new home in El Cajon. The painting will go in the front window of the youth program's Main Street building, which opens Monday.

This program had its times of danger as well. Because we were bringing gang members from different gangs together, there were times when tension was high. We never did have any physical altercations. One incident that happened was an eye opener for us. Our outreach center was located at 445 E. Main Street. I knew the large window facing Main Street made us vulnerable to possible drive-by shootings. To prevent this, we placed a four feet by eight feet sheet of ¾ inch plywood covering the entire window. Some supporters painted the Bridge the Gap logo on the exterior side of the plywood which would face Main St.

I always remained vigilant and alert to any potential signs of danger. One day, I sensed something was wrong. I did not know what, but had a bad feeling. During our boxing training one night, I could see through the front glass door, a van pass by very slowly. I walked around the rear of the building and again saw the van circle around. As it neared the front of the building, the sliding rear door to the van opened, and a Hispanic gang member jumped out with what appeared to be a sawed off shotgun. I immediately yelled at him to stop, at which time he seemed to recognize who I was, although I did not know him. The van sped away and the gang member began to run north across Main Street. I gave chase and called for back up on my portable police radio. I caught up to him and ordered him to the ground to which he complied. He threw the gun down as well. Officer Bill Murphy arrived to assist me in arresting the suspect. The gang member was so stunned that we interrupted his plans and even captured him. This incident seemed to send a strong message on the streets, we have compassion, but we do not play games!

Changed Lives

Other adults in the business community saw the opportunity to change the lives of these young people through Bridge the Gap and joined in mentoring troubled teenagers. Those teenagers are now adults, and their lives are stories of success, meeting challenges and making life changes—many of them now mentor teens in the community and among their relatives to ensure that they stay on the right path. All of them faced adversity and challenges. Later on in this book, you will read some stories of just a few who met those challenges and succeeded. The greatest blessing in my life has been the fact that all of the individuals that I share with you, have stood by my side even until today. We are like a family. Every Sunday morning, we all gather together for a Bible study. I play the guitar, and we all sing songs together. It amazes me to be with these incredible friends, and recall all we had been through together. When I see people from the past, they seem very surprised when I tell them that we are still together walking through life together. You see, for them it was a project of some sort. For me, these guys are my life!

One such person, who was at my side through it all, was Jeff Cramer. Jeff has written the story of how we became acquainted and his recollection of the most trying times of my life. Jeff and I have a unique friendship. We often disagree on things, yet we use that to grow, as iron sharpens iron. Jeff would watch my back when I was not sure who else would. Jeff and I have had our ups and downs, the bottom line, he is there when you need him, and if you need someone to watch your back, no one could compare to Jeff.

I can recall a time when we were taking a group of guy's rock climbing near Mexicali. We did not know that the area we were headed to was known as "Smugglers Gulch". This was a dangerous area of the U.S. Mexico border regions that was very dangerous. In the middle of the night, gunshots rang out, and we realized we had unknown subjects firing their guns toward our camp. I was sleeping in my Bronco and was awaken by Jeff tapping on the window telling me there were suspicious men in our camp area. I thought I was dreaming. I climbed out, and met Jeff. Jeff is a strategist, one of the best. We were responsible for the safety of many. Jeff would devise a plan to safely get us out of this dangerous situation. Jeff had one radio and I had the other. Jeff climbed up a cliff to spot where the subjects were. He radioed me telling me their location and best escape route for our guys. Jeff told me to get the guys to start dismantling our camp and be ready to take off. Meanwhile, I had an 800 megahertz radio system in the Bronco. This radio had a phone patch link in which I could make phone calls. I called the San Diego Sheriff's Department. They dispatched a unit to our location but advised us it might be some time before they would get there. Jeff held the perimeter of our camp to make sure the subjects did not enter back into our area. Meanwhile, I along with the guys took down our camp quicker than one could begin to imagine. We destroyed much of our equipment as the high winds made it difficult to get the equipment taken down.

Soon we were ready to depart. Jeff came back to the camp. He and the guys walked along the Bronco as I headed out of the extreme rough roads only passable by four wheel drive. Finally as we began to clear the dangerous area, we came across a Sheriff's Deputy who was making his way toward the subjects who had been shooting at us. He told us this was a very dangerous area and that many people have been killed by drug smugglers. We left the area thanking God no one was hurt.

Jeff was the person who would endanger himself to protect others. He was my protector and I could clearly see how God had placed him at my side. If ever there is a time when I need protection, Jeff is the man.

Mentoring For Success

Each of the young people we mentored has made huge changes in their life and has done so against great odds. Each of them recognizes the significant support system which was provided to them from Bridge the Gap, which helped them to succeed. Bridge the Gap was instrumental in helping them grow into productive adults, many with families of their own. Without caring adults to help them along the way, their future would have been dark and bleak. Having seen the difference a mentor made in their own lives, many are now actively mentoring other young people to success. By mentoring one young person at a time, that person is changed, and he will go on to change the lives of others. Like ripples in a stream, the positive effects of Bridge the Gap and similar community programs are making a difference in the future of troubled youth everywhere.

It is an incredible time when these guys and their families come over to my place for dinner. They have become the best friends a person could ever hope for. The loyalty they have shown me has allowed  me to grow even now. It is unreal how transparent we all seem to be. To all of us, we are a family with a long history of ups and downs. We walk through life together accepting each others weaknesses and helping each other excel to the next level in our effectiveness.

I was very protective of the guys in which I was mentoring. I can remember a time when David Rios showed up to our Boxing club. His arm was swollen and appeared to have been broken. I can remember seeing a bone protruding like a compound fracture. I asked David what had happened. He told me he fell. I did not believe it. I pressured him into telling me the truth. He finally confided in me that while walking to practice today, a group of gang members jumped him and ripped a gold chain with the letter "D" on it from his neck. His dad had given it to him as a gift. The "D" was for David. I was so angry. I knew how gentle David was and how forgiving he was. He kept telling me that it was okay, and that he forgave the guys. Well, I was not content with that. I loaded him in my vehicle to take him to the hospital. He had told me this happened near the El Cajon High School. I was already nearby, so I asked him if he saw the guys while we were driving to tell me. As I passed a group of El Cajon Dukes gang members that I had recognized, I saw David slouch down in the passenger seat. I could clearly sense that he was afraid, and these were the guys. I said, "David, are these the guys?" "Tell me the truth!" He said under his breath, "Yeah, those are the guys." I pulled over, jumped out and ordered all of the subjects to the ground and called for additional officers to start my way. We ended up arresting the group for strong arm robbery. One of the guys, John Fratt, who had thrown a karate kick at David's arm, was charged with felony battery.

I remember later visiting juvenile hall and seeing the guys who had committed the crime. I talked with them and told them the kind of person David was and that David specifically asked me to tell them he offered his forgiveness. They actually cried when I told them that. They were convicted and sentenced.

In the spring of 2003, an article was written about me in the Volunteer San Diego Magazine titled, "An Officer and a Mentor" written by Jeanna Morlan. Here is an excerpt from this article:

Officer Kevin LaChapelle volunteers his time to gang members and tries to get them off the streets through his mentorship program, Bridging the Gap.

A gunshot echoes through the corridors, bouncing off the lockers that are suppose to hold school books. Students fight students, the society and the system. What happens when they are removed from school?

Most students are given a chance at alternative education schools. If the students are lucky, they may get the chance to meet a man whose role as an officer is to serve and protect. This is a motto that Officer Kevin LaChapelle of the El Cajon Police Department takes seriously on and off duty.

Officer LaChapelle works with Chaparral, Grossmont Union High School Districts (GUHSD) continuation school, and Career Development Center (CDC), under the adult education department of GUHSD. It serves youth from 14-20 years old who are referred to them from Chaparral. The center also recruits those that have dropped out of school. CDC offers their students job preparation and guides them back into an alternative education system that will prove beneficial for the individual student.

He also works with the Summit Program, a county-wide school program that serves high risk youth who have been suspended or expelled from their district high school.

"It is unbelievable as to the influence he has had on our students. You see a kid that wants to be known as a 'tough guy,' but once he's involved with Kevin, you see him start to soften," explained Shelly Marshall, instructor at CDC.

Officer LaChapelle has been a police officer for four years, three of which he has volunteered his time with kids in gangs. "I was resentful towards the kids at first," sighed LaChapelle. After his first six months with the department he was called to the scene of a stabbing, where he got to know the kid involved. "I started to see that being involved with gangs was a way out, it's not their fault, it's the structure of their family life," explained LaChapelle.

Every Friday night LaChapelle can be found holding a Bible study for kids in Juvenile Hall. This all began after LaChapelle arrested a kid for confessing to murder. The boy was put in an observation room in case he attempted suicide. His mother called LaChapelle and asked him to go and pray with her son. "When I got there kids just started coming into the room, pretty soon the whole unit was in the room. I think they were curious to see why a cop was visiting. We all sat down and had a Bible study and prayed'" said LaChapelle in deep recollection. He has been holding Bible studies there ever since.

CHAPTER FIVE

Trouble on the Way

In 1993, something happened that began to drive my career downhill faster than an Olympic bobsled. But looking back, I couldn't have acted differently and lived with myself, even knowing all the pain and heartbreak that followed.

One evening I was dining at Bennigan's with my girlfriend, and our best friends, Jeff and Jodi, when I was approached by one of the police cadets—young people who went on an occasional ride-along with regular police officers and who aspired to join the force one day. The cadet was clearly troubled, and he told me that he was finding it impossible to believe what Officer Michael Kennedy had shared with him—that Kennedy was having sexual relations with an underage girl who was the daughter of one of the department's secretaries.

I immediately had a flashback of the incident when I attended Kennedy's birthday party while I was a rookie. I was invited by my training officer to a birthday party at the Kennedy house. At the time, I did not know who he was, or much about him, but I wanted to be a part of the team, so decided to go. When I arrived at his house, I was surprised right away at the fact that there were three young men about 15-16 years old sitting on the couch in his living room all of which were drinking beer. I asked them how old they were. Each replied, one saying 15 and the others saying 16. I asked who they were with from the party and they said, "Mike Kennedy." I was very troubled by this. I made my way through the house finding many colleagues from the department intoxicated. I tried to just "hang out" and planned to leave soon. One officer asked me if I wanted a beer to which I declined. He kept pushing the issue. He was drunk, and wanted me to be drunk as well. He spilled beer on me a few times as he staggered toward me trying to get me to give in. Finally, he and a few others, in a joking manner, began to wrestle me to the ground. They then tried to pour beer in my mouth. Now, I became seriously mad. I fought to break away telling them I was angry. As I broke free, I made my way to the front door. As I entered into the living room, several female strippers were performing lap dances to many of the guys. I was stunned, disgusted, and mad! I left. The next day, I mentioned what had happened to one of my sergeant's. He seemed irritated, but not surprised. He just shrugged and said the officers needed to grow up.

I now knew that Kennedy probably was capable of such behavior. The law in California makes even consensual sex with a person under 18 a statutory crime—that is, any male or female under 18 in California cannot legally consent to sexual relations, and anyone who does have sex with a minor has committed the crime of rape as a matter of law. All through the remainder of the weekend, I was troubled by what I had heard and I knew that as a matter of conscience, I would have to act and find out whether the allegation was true.

On Monday morning, I did a little research and learned that one of our departmental secretaries, did, indeed, have a daughter in her early teens. I found a moment to speak to her alone and said that I had been given information about which her daughter might know something and asked her for permission to meet with her daughter to ask the girl a few questions. At that point, all I had was an unconfirmed report of what might have happened, so I simply told her that her daughter might be a victim of a crime but that I couldn't elaborate until I had checked out all the facts.

She sat for a moment, looking at me questioningly, and then finally said, "This must be something serious. My daughter's been so upset lately, she's seemed suicidal."

I tried to remain noncommittal, assuring her that I just wanted to ask her daughter a few questions, and received her permission to meet with her at her school.

An Unbelievable Discovery

The secretary had an older daughter who was married to a fellow officer, so I asked him to go with me to her daughter's school. I felt that she might feel more comfortable if her brother-in-law were there to reassure her. We met with her privately in the school office, and we reassured her that she was not in any trouble for anything but knew that she might be afraid to speak. Then in a soft voice, I told her that whatever had happened, it was okay to talk to us about it, and I asked her, "Do you know Officer Michael Kennedy? After she said yes, I could see tears swelling up in her eyes. Then I asked her if anything happened between them that she wanted to talk to me about."

She began to cry, and gradually over the next hour, her story began to unfold. She told me she met Kennedy during a Tang Soo Do class sponsored by the El Cajon Police Department. While at class, Kennedy would make comments to her and on one occasion, gave her his pager number telling her to call him sometime. She could not believe an older guy would be interested in her.

Then it happened. She was feeling light-headed from the drink and had the usual curiosity of most teenage girls about what it would be like to be attractive to a much older adult male. Soon he went from compliments to kissing, and finally forced himself on her. When it was over, he warned her not to tell. In tears, she left, feeling guilty about drinking and feeling also that she had brought the sexual act on herself by accepting his invitation to have a drink.

The next time he called to have her baby-sit, she didn't want to go, but she was afraid to decline. As before, he said his wife was working late and offered her more alcohol. On later visits, he encouraged her to invite a girlfriend over. Afraid to say no to him, she did so. Kennedy's friend, Mike "B" joined him, and soon her friend became engaged in sexual activity with Mike "B". Both the girls were drinking heavily, at the encouragement of Kennedy. At the time I interviewed her, Kennedy along with his friend had been having sex with her and her friend for several months. Mike "B" was in the process of being hired as a police officer himself. On one occasion Kennedy asked the victim how she would feel if his wife walked in with a gun. The victim thought this was very strange for Kennedy to say this. Kennedy's wife was a police officer for the Chula Vista Police Department.

Consequences

When she sobbed out her story and came to the part about Mike "B's" participation, I knew that, indeed, trouble was on the way—and it would be coming *my* way very shortly if I pursued the case. Mike "B" was the son of my immediate supervisor, Lt. "S", and the stepson of her husband, Sgt. "S". I knew the consequences of going forward, but I knew the consequences to the young girls if I didn't. Their lives would be ruined forever if I just let it go. I was angry with the whole law enforcement system in our city! To think that men who were sworn to uphold the law and to protect the community could do this and get away with it was unthinkable!

The victim's brother-in-law was angry, too, but he cautioned me, "Be careful, Kevin. This could have major consequences for you." Trouble or not, I knew I had to follow up on the case.

Conviction

I took the case to the La Mesa Police Department because the crime occurred in their jurisdiction. The La Mesa Police pursued the case to its conclusion. Their findings eventually led to the arrest and conviction of both suspects. During this time, Lt. "S" continued to be my supervisor, and it quickly became clear that doing the right thing would have serious consequences for my career. I had yet to learn just how devastating those consequences would be.

An example of what I was now up against can be evidenced by a letter submitted to the District Attorney's Office. To read the letter that was sent to the District Attorney's Office, see Appendix B. Kennedy's wife was a police officer with the Chula Vista Police Department. A Sergeant from her police department submitted a letter to the District Attorney's Office. The District Attorney was stunned and faxed me a copy wanting me to know that they were rallying other officers on Kennedy's behalf against me. He told me, "This will get ugly for you!" I knew they would come at me with everything and try and destroy my credibility. On a few occasions, officers approached me and made disparaging remarks about why I had gone against a fellow officer.

I was so numbed having witnessed the victim's mother be continually harassed by Lt. "S" who was her immediate supervisor as well as mine. I can recall hearing Lt. "S" telling her that her daughter was a whore! The department did absolutely nothing to stop it. Then Lt. "S" arranged for the city to lay off the mother from her secretary position saying they did not have enough work for her to do. Can you imagine that? I knew this was just the beginning. I would soon begin to face similar retaliation.

CHAPTER SIX

Retaliation Time

After I brought Officer Kennedy's case to officials, also implicating Lt. "S's" son Mike "B" in the rape of the victim and her friend, it didn't take long for Lt. "S" to start making it uncomfortable for me to continue with the Department and to exert subtle pressure on me to leave the Department.

I had been Chief Smith's protégée, thanks to the community service programs I started with his encouragement, and he did his best to protect me when he could. But Chief Smith had his own problems. He had fought long and hard against an entrenched "old guard" who sought to keep his reforms from taking effect. The police administration and police union leadership consistently opposed Chief Smith's plan to restructure the police department and sought to undermine the programs which I was commissioned by the Chief to undertake— this was their way of causing trouble for both of us. If those in the administration within the department could undermine what I did in community outreach, it would reflect badly on Chief Smith, as well as sink my career.

I held a strong power base within the community, too, thanks to the positive image I had built about the role of the police as public servants, and initially, the good will of the community offered some protection from the initial retaliation against me from Lt. "S" and several of her close colleagues.

Campaign Politics

In 1994, I was approached by a group of citizens who asked me to run for a position on the Grossmont Union High School District Governing Board of Education. They told me that they believed there was financial corruption among the District's top officials and wanted someone they could trust on the School Board. I was intrigued by their story, but at first I was reluctant to run for office. With nine other candidates, the field was already crowded. I had never run for office before, and even as a political newcomer, I knew that campaigns were seldom clean. Since I was already struggling with the fallout from the Kennedy case at work, I was concerned that my adversaries in the Department could create major problems for me.

A school teacher Joe Meeker had an incredible impact on my life. Joe was a school teacher at one of the local high schools and also taught weight training. I was introduced to him by the principal and vice principal of the school, Chaparral High School. The principal Barbara Stanley and the Vice Principal Diane Carburry were quite a team. They had a heart for the students. They both felt Joe and I would be a great team in reaching the at-risk youth. Joe and I hit it off right away. Joe was like a father to his students. He was an older guy, but was in great shape, and did not take crap off of anyone. We would forge a very close friendship over the years. He financially supported our boxing program and was very impacting on many people. Joe was instrumental in my running for the school board. Meeker treated the students as if they were his family. He also had a construction business on the side and offered work for students. His sense of humor was unreal. I miss the times he and I shared with the guys.

GROSSMONT UNION HIGH SCHOOL DISTRICT
Governing Board Member
KEVIN LA CHAPELLE
Police Officer/El Cajon Police Department School Liaison Officer/
Founder-Director, Bridge The Gap Youth Program/
Member, San Diego County Juvenile Delinquency Committee

Kevin is an El Cajon Police Officer and is the E.C.P.D School Liaison Officer. His focus is helping teenagers become PRODUCTIVE MEMBERS OF SOCIETY AND HELPING HEAL FAMILIES.

Kevin volunteers time as Founder-Director of BRIDGE THE GAP, a local program for troubled youth.

KEVIN HAS INTERVIEWED THOUSANDS OF YOUTH INCARCERATED AS A RESULT OF GANGS AND DRUGS. He has spent thousands of hours on the streets of San Diego County interacting with these youth and their families. He has been equipping the youth and their families for success during such perilous times.

KEVIN BELIEVES EVERY YOUTH NEEDS STRONG ROLE MODELS, AND THAT THE YOUTH NEED TO BE THE PRIORITY OF EVERY COMMUNITY.

Kevin has received numerous awards for his efforts in redirecting the youth from gangs and drugs. KEVIN IS CONSIDERED AN EXPERT IN THE FIELD OF JUVENILE DELINQUENCY PREVENTION AND INTERVENTION.

KEVIN SUPPORTS AND ENCOURAGES SCHOOLS TO SET-UP EFFECTIVE YOUTH PROGRAMS. His programs show the importance of good family relationships, friends that do not take you down, and educational/vocational goals.

Kevin will work to decrease school drop-outs. HE SUPPORTS MAXIMUM EDUCATIONAL OPPORTUNITIES.

KEVIN WILL WORK FOR THE BEST INTEREST OF STUDENTS, FACULTY, And TAXPAYERS.

Accessible – (phone 526-4300)

CS-5100-2   N SD 249-022

At last, I was persuaded and surprisingly became the leading candidate in the race. When the election was held, I had the highest number of votes of any candidate, outdistancing my closest opponents, both incumbents, by over 4200 votes. The campaign was hard, and in the days just before the election, even my faith became an issue because I was conservative in my views. It hurt that my opponents would make my faith an issue instead of focusing on the problems within the District when the schools were facing serious financial problems, including how to fund millions in needed capital improvements. In that same election, the community had voted down a major bond issue that would have provided badly needed funding for school improvements.

One time after deciding to run for the Grossmont School Board, I went to a local Christian bookstore called Jerusalem Corner. This bookstore was on Broadway in El Cajon. The lady at the counter was an incredible woman. Her name was Delores and she was the sweetest older woman ever. She reminded me of my grandmother. Upon telling her of my decision to run for the board, I remember the look on her face. She told me, "Kevin, you be careful, this will be the greatest battle you have ever faced. I will pray for you," she said. Boy did I need that prayer.

Election night, I went home to bed early. Many asked me, "Why aren't you going to go to Election Central? I told them I would rather be at home and see what happens from there. I was home at about 7:00 PM. Before going to sleep, I prayed and asked God, "If I am to take this responsibility on, please allow me to win by great margins. If I am not to get involved with this, please allow me to lose big time. Nothing in between," I said.

I awoke the next morning to the phone ringing. It was a call from a reporter from the Union Tribune. He wanted my comments on my landslide victory in the school board election. I knew then, the battle would be great.

After winning, I immediately began seeing people trying to court me. "Kevin, how would you like us to send you to a conference in Hawaii? Have you ever been to Hawaii?" The Superintendent of Schools would ask me.

I met with Mike Eddy, a Lieutenant from El Cajon Police Department, and Joe Meeker who would begin to help me strategize on the task at hand. Eddy had been targeted by the school district administration. The Lieutenant on the police department had introduced me to Eddy and told me how they were trying to retaliate against him for his criticism of the administration. Eddy and I are very good friends even to this day. He is a man who never lost sight of his loyalty to friends.

The Lieutenant knew of the corrupt nature, power, and control that Lt. "S", my supervisor, held. The problem was, unfortunately, he did not have any control over the police department. Often times, I wished Jack Smith had put together a leadership team consisting of this Lieutenant, another lieutenant, and two sergeants whom all seemed to have good character. Many within the department cheered me on in uncovering what had been exposed thus far. Unfortunately, when I needed their support the most, they were silent. I never held ill feelings toward them, as I knew they had families to support.

"Conflict of Interest"

Over the next few months, I learned that the fears of the citizens who had encouraged me to run were well founded—and there was more. As part of my investigation into other financial matters, I discovered that money for one of the school's federally funded programs had been misappropriated.

My victory in the election stirred up more animosity within the Police Department and among entrenched opposition already on the School Board. They did everything possible to destroy my credibility and to thwart my success.

As soon as I was seated on the Board, Lt. "S" and her colleagues asserted that my serving on the Board was a conflict of interest with my role in the Department. I was suddenly an elected public official as well as a Police Officer, where much of my work was with gangs in local schools, trying to help these young people turn their lives around. I was advised by the Department's administration that because I was working with gangs in the local schools, I would be transferred to a different position in the Department where I would not have a "perceived conflict of interest" with my position as a Governing Board member.

To make matters worse, Chief Smith had resigned from the Department, tired of fighting for the badly needed reforms, sadly acknowledging defeat in his attempt to reorganize the Department and eliminate the corruption that had persisted for years. Chief Smith accepted an Under-Sheriff's position with the San Diego Sheriff's Department. As soon as he resigned, Lt. "S" and her colleagues stepped up their retaliation against me. To them, I had become a renegade, breaking the unwritten code of silence to protect others on the Force, even if they were engaging in wrongdoing.

I received death threats and had credible sources within the police department advise me that the administration had been holding strategy sessions. The sole topic discussed was how to "get rid of LaChapelle". They also were doing everything they could to "find dirt" on me; to no avail.

One night, I received a phone call from a lieutenant. He asked me to meet him at a local park. He asked me to come alone. I trusted this lieutenant, however in light of the threats against me, was a little reluctant. I called my friend Jeff and asked him to follow me and keep an eye on what transpired. He would basically provide cover for me during this meet. After I knew Jeff was in the area, I drove into the parking lot of Hillside Park. I noticed a city vehicle in the parking lot which belonged to the lieutenant. I saw the lieutenant in the center

LaChapelle big GUHSD winner

Olsen, Mott also re-elected

By Lori Arnold
Daily Californian staff writer

LA MESA — When Kevin LaChapelle is sworn in next month as the newest member of the Grossmont Union High School District governing board, he and his colleagues will be trying to figure out how to fund millions in needed capital improvements after a proposed bond measure went down to defeat.

LaChapelle, who earned 38,543 votes, or 16.22 percent in Tuesday's contest, will join incumbents Maynard Olsen and June Mott, who easily won re-election. LaChapelle emerged as the leader early on in the contest and never lost his edge. Olsen, who garnered 34,261 votes, or 14.42 percent and Mott, who captured 32,840 votes or 13.82 percent, were also at the top but switched standings about halfway through the night. LaChapelle will fill the seat vacated by Tom Davies, who upset long-time incumbent Marty Block on the County Board of Education.

Mott, an educator for more than four decades, will begin her third term in December, while Olsen will begin his second. LaChapelle said he was excited to be elected with the incumbents, both of whom he said he had tremendous respect for.

LaChapelle, involved in his first run at public office, said he wasn't sure how he would do with such a crowded field. He said in the waning days of the campaign his religion became an issue.

"I'm not going to do a Vista school board thing," he said, referring to dissension on the North County board that resulted in two members of the religious right being recalled Tuesday night. "When it came out people saying that about me, I thought it would hurt me."

Proposition O, which would have provided up to $75 million to upgrade aging schools and build additional facilities to house up to 8,000 more students in the next decade, earned more than enough votes to win a simple majority, but failed to pass the required

GROSSMONT SCHOOL BOARD ★ ★

K. La Chapelle	**38,543**
Maynard Olsen	**34,261**
June Mott	**32,840**
Robert Chatham	28,995
Vallera Johnson	26,481
S. Wolfe-Fleming	25,608
Guy Halgren	21,821
Mark Montijo	12,797
Raymond Peters	9,624
Bruce Johnson	6,653

LaChapelle, involved in his first run at public office, said he wasn't sure how he would do with such a crowded field. He said in the waning days of the campaign his religion became an issue.

two-thirds majority.

Although the 57 percent yes vote was significant, especially in an anti-tax climate, the defeat was stinging to district officials who lobbied hard for its passage. Volunteers spend hundreds of hours speaking before service clubs and promoting the plan through the PTA.

Mike Harrelson, who sits on the Grossmont governing board, said he was obviously disappointed but that the district will have to try again.

"A large majority of the voters out there are in favor of the Grossmont Union district," he said. "I don't know how we are going to deal with overcrowding and the aging facilities, especially when the state now longer has the money and the legislators don't have the will. I don't know where we're going to get the money to build new school or add new classrooms."(lla-de) area of the park near a picnic table. I walked over to him. He began to tell me that he believed in me and really liked me, but that he was scared I was going to get hurt. He basically told me that I needed to be careful and that there were discussions on how to deal with me. He asked me if I knew how much power Lt. "S" wielded, to which I acknowledged I did. He ended our conversation by saying, "Kevin, watch your back, and be careful!" I then met with Jeff and told him what had transpired. The next day, Jeff, his wife, myself and my girl went to the same park and prayed together. Jeff began to share with me that he had a very sick feeling inside that something might happen to me. We prayed asking for God's protection and for Him to bring the corrupt police department to justice one day.

One of their first big moves after the Chief's resignation was to assign me to the Vice Squad as an undercover officer. I was forced to continue in this assignment for six months and in many little ways, the other officers made it clear that they would not watch my back if I found myself in trouble. They tried repeatedly to find anything negative they could use against me, but I knew they would find nothing.

Undercover Vice

In about January of 1995, I was reassigned to an undercover vice assignment. This was a classic bait and switch. Lt. "S" advised me that due to the perceived conflict of interest of my being a police officer and also an elected public official, I was pressured to put in for a transfer to a new position which would be educating the public on the dangers of alcohol. The Lieutenant told me how my being certified as a DARE Officer would help me in this new position. I had a feeling something was not quite right, but did not know until later that the position was changed to an undercover vice position.

The police administration clearly knew that I would have an issue with frequenting strip clubs, prostitutes and being exposed to cigarette smoke to which I was seriously allergic too. At the time smoking was not prohibited in bars. I did everything I could to deal with this new assignment. I wanted to just get through it as I valued my job as a police officer and did not want to resign. I knew they were doing everything in their power in hopes of pushing me into resigning, however I would not budge.

The next step the lieutenant took was to assign me to the San Diego Police Department's Vice Unit for some "training". During my assignments with their unit, it was probably the toughest assignment ever. I was told that I would wear a U.S. Navy ball cap and act is if I were in the military. My job, to see how close I could get to touching strippers in the clubs because the City of San Diego had a municipal code which required a certain distance remain between strippers and patrons. I would work tandem with two other undercover officers. They would urge me to consume alcohol so I would fit in. Otherwise, they hinted, I would risk my safety of having my cover blown. These guys consumed beer after beer. I was stunned that no controls seemed to be in place for the officers. It was almost a free for all at the expense of the city.

Other assignments included hanging out at bars trying to pick up on prostitutes. Checking out the local "F" Street bookstores, and going to the x-rated movies. I had never in my life been exposed to so much trash. This would have a huge impact on my life. Being exposed to the pornography would put imprints in my mind that at times would play like slide shows. There were times when I would lay down to go to sleep, and these pornographic images would haunt me. Fortunately, God would later bring a person into my life that would help me heal these scars.

On one occasion, I had enough. I walked to a pay phone and called my girlfriend to come and pick me up. I was so disgusted with everything. I was very angry having known that the lieutenant knew very well what she was exposing me to, and I knew it was intentional. I finally had enough, and demanded a transfer back to patrol.

Saying Goodbye

In mid-1995, Lt. "S" told me that if I were to return to the patrol division, I would be required to work Thursday evenings—the same night the School Board met. My shift would be 6:00 PM to 6:00 AM. By then I was making headway into the financial irregularities that the citizens who had asked me to run for the Board had told me they suspected. The fate of the schools in any community impacts the future of the children and the whole community's future. With funds being misused, I knew that my greatest obligation was where I could do the greatest good. And, sadly, I also knew that there was nothing more I could do within the Police Department because the harassment and retaliation would continue unless the Department underwent a major overhaul. With Chief Smith gone, that was not likely to happen.

I resigned from the El Cajon Police Department in order to continue my work on the School Board and soon thereafter filed a lawsuit against the Police Department for their retaliation against me. Depositions were taken, and among them was a statement by former Police Chief Jack Smith, stating that he had concerns for my safety, recalling meetings conducted by other high ranking officers in which they discussed ways to "neutralize" me. However, the federal judge who heard the case would not allow Chief Smith's statement into evidence, nor would he agree to admit hundreds of other documents submitted. The judge granted a summary judgment in favor of the City of El Cajon. Meaning, the case never even got before a jury. The judge threw the case out citing no evidence, yet, he refused any of the evidence we tried to submit. I entered an appeal of the case, but the City threatened to seek thousands of dollars in attorneys' fees if I pursued the case to the next level. Reluctantly, I dismissed my appeal. The police department still to this day tries to tarnish my reputation anytime they find opportunity.

During the lawsuit, documents were filed in court outlining my evaluations and awards while a police officer. I include this information to articulate that prior to going against the grain, my reputation was impeccable. As soon as I took a stand, you would have thought I was the worst officer in the world. For a detailed account of my performance evaluations, see Appendix C.

One year after I left the department, two El Cajon Police Officers and a Los Angeles Police Officer all were killed in a murder suicide. An El Cajon Police Officer was having a relationship with a police officer from Los Angeles. They were in the midst of breaking up. The Los Angeles Officer came down to La Mesa, California to pick up his belongings from his now ex-girlfriends home. The female had another El Cajon Police Officer who had stayed the night with her. When the Los Angeles Officer saw this, he became enraged, shot and killed the male El Cajon officer, chased the female El Cajon officer around the house, finally shooting and killing her. The Los Angeles officer then turned the gun on himself committing suicide. My brother who was a Detective with the La Mesa Police Department was working his last day on the job when he got the call to this crime scene. He then retired and pursued a career in the insurance business.

I knew that the Department would always haunt me in trying to destroy me. For example, in 2001, I applied for a position as a Special Agent for the California Department of Justice. After passing the polygraph examination, I was called in for a secondary interview. During this interview, one of the investigators advised me that he had spoken with my former supervisor with whom he was close friends with. Needless to say, I was no longer considered for that position.

Several other Officers have alleged corruption even as recently as 2004 within the El Cajon Police Department. One Officer who brought forth major allegations of corruption was retaliated upon severely. He and his wife were subjected to a false anonymous tip alleging money laundering in which the FBI conducted a raid of their home. Later the FBI acknowledged the information had been provided by top level officials at the El Cajon Police Department, and that the information later was confirmed to be totally false and without merit. That Officer has pending litigation against the City of El Cajon for this incident.

Going Forward

Was I angry? You bet! I was angry at the Police Department that allowed corrupt officers to remain on the force. I was angry at the judge who refused to consider the case fairly. I was even angry with God and spent a lot of time feeling that there was no reward for doing the right thing, for working to better the community, and for losing the career on which I had embarked with such high hopes. In the months that followed, I spent a lot of time feeling hurt and abandoned for choosing to do what was right instead of going along with the bad guys in the Department. Why should I have to suffer? My anger was greater because Kennedy and Mike "B", the two on whom I'd blown the whistle the year before were serving out a very minimal sentence at their homes under electronic surveillance instead of going to prison. I was angry that my former Lieutenant got a promotion to Captain. I was the one who had to give up a career I loved and they were all still prospering. Where was the justice in that? How could God let this happen to me? It took me months to regain my focus and realize that God must have a purpose for me in all that I was going through. And it's a good thing that I did get over my anger, because my work as a Trustee on the School Board was going to take all the attention I had to give in the months ahead. It was time now to look forward, not back, and see what God had in store for me next.

The lessons were great. I learned how important it is for the leadership of an organization to be centered on principles. If they are self centered instead of principally centered, their every decision is skewed and based on self interest instead of the interest of what is right. I also would learn more about myself and my flaws. God wanted me to see that He was awesome, not me!

CHAPTER SEVEN

Cleaning House at the School District

Even before I left the El Cajon Police Department, the School District's problems were coming to light as I began investigating the financial corruption. Among these was the misuse of funds at the District's Career Development Center, where students aged 14 to 22 received career training through a federally funded Job Training Partnership Act (JTPA) program. The Center's program made it possible for high-risk students, those who had been in gangs, and high school dropouts to return to school and receive career training so they could find productive jobs.

During my investigation, the suspect, a supervisor at the Center, came to the Police Department and asked to meet with me. She acknowledged that she had in fact diverted school funds for her personal use and planned to resign from her post and withdraw her retirement funds to make restitution, and she signed a statement during the meeting describing what she had done. At least 77 checks, totaling over $3,000 had been endorsed to her by students at her request. The JTPA provided allowances for the students for their lunches, bus passes, even haircuts, so they could find work. The checks represented money the students badly needed in order to find employment. The employee admitted that she would get the students to endorse the checks over to her, and she would give them cash back for their lunches each day, keeping part of the funds for herself. However, one student said that sometimes when lunchtime came, the employee was gone, and the student couldn't buy lunch that day and went without.

A number of students suspected something was wrong, but whenever they confronted the supervisor, she always either gave an evasive reply or told them it was none of their business. After the employee admitted to her wrongdoing, I brought the findings to the School District, which hired a San Diego accounting firm to audit the Center's program. Although controls were implemented to prevent this misuse of funds from occurring again—the supervisor resigned and made restitution—there was more to come in the months ahead.

Upon being elected to the governing board of education, fellow board member Dr. Maynard Olson, a medical doctor in private practice, was now serving a second school board term. He began to share with me that he knew something was seriously wrong within the school district. He suspected financial kickbacks and bid rigging. The other board members which formed a solid voting block of three were June Mott, Ada Reap, and Mike Harrelson. They were responsible for giving the former superintendent JoAnn Smith and Fred Martinez a rubber stamp to do whatever they wanted with no accountability whatsoever.

Maynard would share with me the modus operandi of this three board majority and how they seemed to thwart his every effort to bring these wrongdoings to light. He told me how frustrated he was. He began sharing with me many incidents that had occurred over his tenure on the board. He told me of times that his doctor's office had been boycotted by the teachers union. He eventually moved out of state and did not seek reelection.

By 1996, I had served two years on the Board, pursuing and uncovering evidence of fraud and financial mismanagement, every step of the way hindered by the Superintendent JoAnn Smith, and Director of Business Services, Fred Martinez. My "reward" for my efforts was a series of vicious attacks in the local newspapers, maligning my reputation however they could. The teachers union was closely aligned with Superintendent Smith and the Finance Director Fred Martinez, whose activities I was investigating. The administration and union leadership did everything possible to prevent me from accessing the documents I needed to uncover the truth. At one point they even censured me and orchestrated a meeting with hundreds in attendance to dissuade me from continuing the investigation. Fortunately, scores of members of the community attended the meeting as well and supported my efforts.

On another occasion, concerned parents Bruce Johnson and Chris Meinsen had asked me to accompany them to a special education school within the district over allegations of the district failing to comply with American with Disabilities Act (ADA) federal laws. I agreed. Upon entering the school, we were greeted by one of the administrative staff members. I advised them why I was there and asked if we could inspect the site. I had a tape recorder with me in which I would use for accurate note taking to insure the facts of the investigation were accurate. The administrative official began to get belligerent with us. At this time I held up the tape recorder in plain view and turned the switch on. It was obviously on as a red light now illuminated showing it was recording. The official could clearly see the recorder being turned on. He ordered us out of the school. This was interesting, because the school was one of the many within my jurisdiction in my capacity of an elected governing board member.

The next thing I knew, I received a call from the San Diego Sheriff's Department advising me that the school official had called them and reported that they wanted me arrested for burglary. "Burglary!" I was stunned. The Deputy told me that the official said I had tape recorded him without his permission which was a crime. I explained to the Deputy as to what had transpired. The law states that you cannot tape record someone without their knowledge. The official obviously had knowledge or they would not have known I was recording them in the first place. The Deputy did not seem to care as to our side of the incident and was more intent on arresting me. I told him I would be calling a press conference and turning myself in so he could take me into custody. When I said this, he stuttered and seemed a little nervous that I would be calling a press conference. Bruce Johnson and Chris Meinsen were flabbergasted at best. The Sheriff's Deputy elected not to arrest me and instead said they would be referring the case to the District Attorney's Office for review. The next day in the newspaper on the front page read the following headline, "LaChapelle charged with Burglary". You cannot imagine the phone calls I received. What is going on, they would ask. Later the District Attorney said there was insufficient evidence to charge me so the charges were dismissed.

In yet another incident, I received a call from an irate father who demanded to know why a racist like me was on a school board. I was stunned to hear this. He demanded a meeting with me to which I agreed. We met at a local restaurant where he began to tell me that he called the school district upset over two of his Spanish speaking children not being taught English. He then explained that he was on the bilingual advisory committee for the school district. When he called the district to complain, they forwarded his call to Assistant Superintendent Carl Wong. Wong told him that there was a particular board member who was responsible for the Latino students not being held accountable to learn English. Wong then went on to tell this man that I was that board member, and that I was against the Latino community.

I brought with me to this meeting with the parent a photo album to show this parent of my involvement with the Latino community. It did not take long for this parent to be even more outraged, not at me, but at Carl Wong for being dishonest and trying to turn this parent against me without any merit whatsoever. After this meeting, I drove to the district office to meet with Carl Wong to find out why he told this parent what he did. Bruce Johnson, another concerned parent in the district, accompanied me as I did not want to meet alone without a witness due to the continual attacks I was under. As we entered Wong's office he invited us in. As we sat down and began to explain what had happened in the meeting with the parent, Wong grew outraged and ordered us out of his office. As we were leaving, he was pushing his door closed and caught my foot in it. He then locked the door and we left.

I then received a call from the El Cajon Police Department telling me that they were investigating a crime in which parent Bruce Johnson and I assaulted Carl Wong in his office. I was stunned. Here we go again. It was never ending as to their malicious tactics. Later that night I received a call from a reporter. The reporters wife was a school teacher in the Grossmont High School District. He asked me what kind of a truck I drove. I was confused as to why he would ask me such a question. I advised him I do not drive a truck, it is a Ford Bronco. He said, "That is considered a truck, isn't it?" I told him maybe and asked why he was asking? He said never mind and hung up the phone. The next day I awoke and read a front page article with the story starting like this: "Truck driven, buzz cut LaChapelle, from Lakeside...." The article began to tell the story of what happened with Carl Wong and my allegedly assaulting him. Interestingly, I have never resided in Lakeside, however they were trying to paint me as a redneck racist. Most readers did not buy it as they knew of my commitment to the Latino community. I later found out that the reporter's wife was not only a school teacher in the Grossmont District, but she was heavily involved in the union.

With all this pressure brought to bear, did I think of giving up? That would have been easy, but I would have to live with myself and know that if I abandoned the investigation, the schools would be worse off than before, and I would have lost all sense of integrity. I was grateful for the support from the community, and that gave me strength to keep on doing what I knew had to be done.

Threats and Bribes

One afternoon in September 1996, I received a page on my voicemail pager. An unknown male caller had left me a threatening message, saying: "Hey, Chapelle, if you keep this shit up with the Grossmont District, I'm going to put a fucking bullet through your head. You understand? You better back off, pal. Bastard!" I didn't recognize the voice but filed a complaint with the San Diego Sheriff's Department, who had jurisdiction. Of course, without any idea of who was calling, the police could do nothing, but I wanted the incident on record in case anything further happened. I certainly couldn't tie the call to anyone on the School Board or anyone who might have attended the meetings. Yet I strongly suspected that the caller was somehow involved in the financial corruption in the District which I was continuing to investigate.

The Investigation Heats Up

Superintendent JoAnn Smith resigned her position in 1996, amid allegations of financial fraud, and was replaced by Dr. Thomas A. Godley in April 1997. Interestingly, during the selection of the new superintendent, many candidates appeared to be ready and willing to take on the corruption in the school district. The choice was so difficult to know who was legitimate and who was planted by JoAnn Smith to continue to cover her trail. I recall telling a fellow board member, "Let's just pray for a godly man. After I had said that, in walks Dr. Thomas "Godley" for his interview. Coincidence? I later learned this was divine.

Godley remained cautious of all politics and settled into his position as new Superintendent of GUSHD. I turned over my investigation to him as I believed he was trustworthy. He definitely felt there were serious issues with the school district finances. He had previous experience in uncovering fraud in a district previous to this one.

As soon as the district realized Godley was uncovering even more improprieties, they began to come after him and his new administration with a vengeance. Godley brought in a great team of individuals. Ron Anderson was his Assistant Superintendent, his right hand man. Ron had incredible character and wisdom. Bill Walk was the Assistant Superintendent of Human Resources. Bill had a passion for his work, he was a perfectionist. They brought Mike Eddy to the

FBI probe Grossmont District finances

By Isaac H. Cubillos

In what seems to be a never-ending saga of intrigue, Latino Beat has been able to confirm that the FBI has been looking into the allegations of illegal activity uncovered by the two audits done last year.

The audits conducted by Vavrinek, Trine, Day & Co., LLP, and Deloitte & Touche, LLP focused on the district's business services division. Both reports identified key findings of deficiencies in the district's internal control system.

According to sources at the district, the FBI began its investigation in January shortly after being contacted by the district by an employee of Deloitte.

Documents obtained show that Todd Fenner, a certified fraud investigator working for the auditing firm, approached the district with information that "certain significant irregularities" were not addressed in the Deloitte & Touche report.

It is said that federal investigators have copied hundreds of financial and other district documents over the past six months for examination.

The first public mention of the FBI's probe reportedly when Trustee Kevin LaChapelle and former Trustee Nadia Davies said that the district was under federal scrutiny.

Trustee Michael Harrelson said, until recently, he was in the dark about the investigation. However, he did confirm that the FBI has been collecting district documents.

"Dr. Godley told me," said Harrelson. "But, he would not disclose what the nature of the investigation."

The district's finances were called into question when the audits uncovered that illegal bidding for contracts was being done to circumvent the law.

Additionally, the district's financial officer, Fred Martinez stopped presenting monthly financial reports to the governing board during the time that the district had significant deficit spending.

According the district, Martinez had misrepresented critical financial information regarding the refinancing of the Certificates of Participation for the Steele Canyon High School Construction Project.

He had failed to fully disclose the actual fees paid to California Financial Services. CFS refused to cooperate with Deloitte auditors and would not provided them with financial disclosures. According to sources, the FBI has contacted CFS.

Records show that on the day that Martinez abandoned his job, he checked out a district vehicle and drove to the San Juan Capistrano offices of CFS.

Harrelson said that the last time he spoke to Martinez was the day before he left the district.

"It was a surprise to me when I heard he had abruptly left," said Harrelson. "I don't know why he left nor have I had contact with him since then."

Harrelson said it would be speculative to make anything of Martinez' trip to CFS.

Trustee June Mott said in a telephone interview that it's been several months since she's had contact with Martinez.

"I think that an honest man is being trashed," said Mott.

According to Fenner, Harrelson made an $80,000 mortgage payment in 1992, however, the source of the funds could not be located.

Harrelson responded to the veiled accusation by saying that any attempt to read into the money would be seriously be taking out of context the facts.

"I did a number of refinancing of my house to get the lower interest rates that were available then," said Harrelson. "This, I'm sure is available in public documents at county, and I find it difficult to think they were unable to uncover this."

district office as well. Mike had the background information with the district to help overcome its challenges. They forged a strong cabinet ready to restructure the district. Unfortunately, the old guard was not going to allow that to happen no matter what.

In the months ahead, other, more subtle pressure was brought to bear—if I couldn't be scared away from pursuing the financial corruption on the School Board, maybe I could be bribed. Fellow board member Michael Harrelson called me on the phone asking if I would agree to meet him for lunch. He said he thought he knew of a way in which we could work together on something that would be mutually beneficial.

Auditing the funds of the Grossmont District would prove extremely difficult. With an annual budget of over $118 million dollars, one would think that the accounting would be maintained on a computer. However, Martinez maintained all records on ledgers in pencil. Auditors found erasures throughout the documents which made it incredibly difficult to audit. In addition, many computer records were immediately deleted and entire hard drives destroyed.

The FBI had already contacted me on a few occasions advising me that they were conducting an investigation; however, I could not disclose this to the public. I called one of the Special Agents to advise him of the phone call from Harrelson. They asked me if I would agree to wear a wire to record what transpired during the meeting to which I agreed. I met with them and they placed the body wire on me.

I met Harrelson at Pizza Nova in La Mesa. He acted very nervous and actually asked me several times if I was recording him. He joked at one point and said, "If you are, and don't tell me, you can get in a lot of trouble." I just laughed and assured him that I was not recording him. He then began to tell me that many of his friends in the district were being unfairly targeted by the investigation Godley was now pursuing. He wanted me to help him get rid of Godley, and then bring back the old guard. If I would agree to work with him, he could get people to back off of me. I played stupid and just listened. He went on to tell me that he felt he and I could be a good team. He seemed reluctant at times to talk as he appeared to be certain I was recording him.

I left and then went directly to the school district office as he did because we had a board meeting. As I entered into one of the offices, the FBI agent and I were in the restroom where he removed the wire. As he was doing this, one of the secretaries knocked on the door and advised me that Harrelson was outside and looking for me. The FBI Agent put the wire back on me, and I exited the restroom while the Agent continued to hide in the restroom.

Harrelson saw me and asked if I would come outside of the office for a moment as he wanted to speak with me. I did so. Harrelson began to tell me that he wanted to get rid of Superintendent Godley tonight during the closed session meeting. He told me that he had already met with other board members and he just needed my support. He was angry that Godley was pressing on with audits targeting the school district finances. He told me that if I put a stop to the investigation into District's finances, and agreed to fire Godley, he could stop the retaliation from the El Cajon Police Department against me—he could "make it go away." He said he had a close friend on the El Cajon City Council, Todd Keegan, who already agreed to Harrelson that he would help stop my ongoing "troubles" and even get me reinstated back onto the police department. I was stunned at this blatant attempt by Harrelson and his arrogance. I then met the FBI Agent back in the restroom so he could retrieve his device. I told him of the exchange with Harrelson, and he just smiled and said, "Let them sink themselves".

I was so incensed at Harrelson's new found fight to rid the district of Dr. Godley because of his uncovering the dirty deeds. Tom Godley was a great man with integrity and exactly what the district needed. Godley was not a yes man; he was very independent and would stick to his principals at all cost. I learned so much from him in such a short amount of time. I watched him lead other men and how they were awed at his leadership. I could see how much Godley inspired them to do the right thing. I enjoyed watching them all work together. They all had incredible trust between one another and remained focused to the task at hand; make this the best district ever!

Now the board had a new majority of which supported me in my efforts, elected me as the new President of the Governing Board, and staunchly supported newly appointed Dr. Thomas Godley. Our commitment was specifically to bring integrity and honor back into the school district and implement controls to insure that the financial mismanagement would be a thing of the past.

Shortly after he assumed his duties as Superintendent, Dr. Godley met with Fred Martinez, Director of Business Services and chief financial officer for the District, requesting a briefing on the financial condition of the District. When Martinez left Superintendent Godley's office, he never returned to his office and fled without a trace. Of course, this intensified our investigation into the District's financial affairs. We later learned that as soon as Martinez left Superintendent Godley's office, he checked out a District vehicle and drove to the Carlsbad, California, offices of California Financial Services (CFS), a company which allegedly provided school facility planning, financial planning, state funding, and administrative support services to the District, for which the District had paid CFS $750,000. However, there are no records in the District to support that those services were ever actually received, and insiders told me they had never performed any services to the district.

Subsequent research revealed that there were many irregularities in the financial administration of the District's affairs—and these had been going on for years! Just a few of the appalling problems uncovered from the years of Superintendent JoAnn Smith's and Director Fred Martinez' administration were gradually revealed during the investigation:

- The District had not complied with statutory requirements and legal advice concerning ensuring fair practices in competitive bidding. Evidence suggested that kickbacks were routine with vendors.

- In 1994-95, the District had transferred over $500,000 from the Deferred Maintenance Fund to its General Fund without the Governing Board's approval as required by law.

- From 1991 through 1997, the District's reserves were below the statutory requirements when it closed its books each year.

- In July 1992, the Business Services Division stopped presenting monthly financial reports to the Governing Board, coinciding with significant deficit spending by the District from July 1992 through June 1995.

- The Business Services Division—again under Martinez' administration—significantly understated the actual costs paid to California Financial Services (CFS) from 1989 through 1997. Martinez asserted to the board that between $40,000.00 and $250,000.00 was paid to CFS. Actually figures totaled $754,093.00. FBI had been conducting separate investigations against CFS involving other school districts. Grossmont had no documentation of any services provided to CFS.

- In January 1997, Martinez misrepresented critical financial information regarding refinancing of Certificates of Participation for the Steele Canyon High School construction project, resulting in the District's spending $18 million in unnecessary refinancing. In addition, California Financial Services would have received an additional $600,000 in fees if newly appointed Superintendent Godley had not acted quickly to cancel the contract with CFS.

"The Worst Government Entity I've Ever Seen..."

An investigative audit of the Grossmont Union High School District's finances was conducted by Deloitte & Touche. When the audit was completed in early

January 1998, Investigative Auditor Todd Fenner contacted me saying that a number of serious discrepancies were found during the audit, and he believed there was evidence of criminal activity. Fenner explained that some findings hadn't been in Deloitte's final report because he had been unable to gain access to all the documents needed to conduct a thorough investigation; nevertheless, he felt we should know about them and follow up. He wanted to meet with me and the District's Legal Counsel to discuss his findings. At that time, I was serving as President of the Governing Board, and called a meeting with Todd Fenner, our Legal Counsel, Mark Bresee, and Superintendent Thomas A. Godley. Everything we had suspected was true—and worse!

An auditor who investigates potential fraud has to be both a detective and a forensic accountant, with the ability to track down clues hidden in financial information and property records, and Todd Fenner proved himself to be an ace in both areas! As soon as our meeting with Todd convened, he began reviewing his findings with us, starting with the activities of Fred Martinez. Fenner told us that there was no listing in the public records of Martinez owning any real estate, although his ownership was, in fact, known. Two condominiums owned by Martinez were shown on property records as being owned, respectively, by "Jack Rice" and "H&H," a real estate investment firm located in La Mirada. H&H Investments' involvement had raised an immediate red flag for Fenner because the Grossmont School District leased facilities owned by H&H for some of its adult school programs. This meant that Martinez had a serious conflict of interest between his role as Director of Business Services where he had control over acquisition of leased properties for the District and his affiliation and possible ownership of H&H. Fenner had visited the two condominiums, and in both cases, the person who answered the door said that Martinez did not live there. However, when Fenner sent certified documents to both those addresses, the return receipts showed that "Mr. Martinez" had signed for both packages.

Fenner also found that the reimbursement records of Martinez' travel and conference expenses revealed that he routinely paid for all reimbursable expenses in cash instead of by credit card or check. This looked suspiciously like Martinez had tried deliberately to ensure that there was no paper trail of his travel expenses, if indeed, he had spent the money. By the time we met, Martinez had been missing for almost nine months and attempts to locate him had been fruitless.

When Fenner contacted California Financial Services, the company that Martinez visited the day he disappeared, Michael Ogburn, head of the company, suggested that Martinez may have "skipped town with some of the refinancing money for the Steele Canyon High School project"—the same project for which

Martinez had falsely told the School Board had to be refinanced a few months earlier.

I recalled a strange dinner meeting a year earlier with Martinez and Bruce Johnson at Bennigan's Restaurant, during the time that JoAnn Smith was still Superintendent. Martinez was discussing the library systems, hinting at some serious irregularities and indicated that he would have more information at their next meeting. When I ran into Martinez a few days later, he had bruises around both eyes and said they were the result of a racquet ball accident, but to me, the bruises looked more as if Martinez had been beaten. He behaved nervously when we spoke and said that he had been ordered by Superintendent Smith to no longer talk to me.

Fenner next moved to a discussion of Warren Williams, Director of Computers & Technology Services for the District. Both Williams and Martinez had been involved in purchasing a very expensive Docutec Xerox machine. Williams said it was bought to replace outdated copy machines at school sites, but upon investigating, Fenner found that none of the old machines had been replaced. Williams also told Fenner that the Docutec would be used to photocopy certain textbooks, and Fenner advised us that photocopying the books would be a violation of federal Copyright laws.

Fenner investigated Williams' computer hard drive, but all the information on it had been "scrambled"—the documents on it had been overwritten to avoid their being read, and Fenner believed that Williams did this to deliberately destroy records. Fenner told us in the meeting that as soon as the Deloitte & Touche report was released, Williams' attorney sent Deloitte & Touche a letter claiming that Williams' reputation had been "blackened" and that the report implied that Williams "was a crook." Additionally, after Williams resigned from the district, evidence was found that he was still accessing district computer information and deleting files remotely.

I recalled in the meeting that I had heard allegations that some of the contractors who did work for the District were doing grading on undeveloped land owned by Williams on which he later built a custom home for over half a million dollars. There was a serious question as to whether Williams had appropriately paid these vendors and what conflict of interest his using them might involve.

The final part of Fenner's report to us concerned asset searches on all board members. Michael Harrelson, who had tried to bribe me to give up the investigation, had made an $80,000 mortgage payment in 1992, but no source for the funds could be located. Shortly thereafter in the same year, Harrelson then refinanced the same property. Harrelson's conflict of interest form, required to be filed by all board members, made no mention of any source of the funds. When matters became public soon after our meeting, Harrelson was questioned by the media but waived the matter away, saying he had been refinancing his home to get lower interest rates, and refused to discuss it further.

Fenner said that the District's Director of Transportation Services, James MacElligott, refused to speak with any of the Deloitte & Touche auditors without his attorney present. MacElligott, had sold a software program to the school district for pupil transportation scheduling and made thousands of dollars, while failing to complete a conflict of interest disclosure as required by law. He summed up his report by saying that the Grossmont District was among the worst government entities he had ever audited because there were virtually no internal controls. The lack of documentation and a clear audit trail meant that there was a strong possibility that fraud and kickbacks had taken place for years. He also believed that the lack of internal controls was deliberate in order to avoid any tracking by a later audit. At that point, Deloitte & Touche could go no further without documents that had been withheld or were possibly missing.

Superintendent Godley and I agreed that these findings were probably the tip of the iceberg and that we had a long road ahead of us to get to the truth. Since the District lacked a general subpoena power to obtain the needed records, it was time to call in an outside resource to help us—one that was unconnected to the City of El Cajon.

Time for a Change

Two days after that meeting, working with Superintendent Godley, I contacted the FBI and requested that the Bureau initiate a formal fraud investigation into the District's affairs, explaining that the District lacked the general subpoena power required to get all the documents needed to prove the wrongdoing in court. As a result of the investigation, the entire School District Administration's officials were eventually replaced, and safeguards were established to ensure accountability in the School District in the future. Martinez has never been found. Now at least, the District could start again, this time with a clean slate.

The work I had set out to do for the District had been accomplished, and it felt good to succeed there where I had been unable to do so in the Police Department. But the last unhappy years on the police force and the struggle to rid the District School Board of the financial corruption that had persisted over many years had taken a huge toll on me financially, and emotionally. I was proud of what I had accomplished, but decided not to seek re-election after my term expired in 1998. It was time for a new challenge, time to find a new way of being of service to others…in short; it was time to move on. That new challenge was waiting just ahead.

Throughout my time on the school board, I would be blessed beyond measure with an attorney whom would later become one of my most treasured friends. Carl and I had a unique friendship. We generally disagreed during many discussions. One thing the both of us did agree on was standing up for what is right. Carl was a pillar to me. Of course he would get irritated with me when I did not follow his legal advice, but we were always able to laugh about it. Carl has been instrumental in representing our non-profit organization to help countless individuals who had been scammed or taken advantage of. Carl and his wife Lisa are quite a team, and an example as to what a strong marriage should be, which is a man and a woman who can call each other best friends.

The Integrity of Tom Godley and His Team

I chose not to run for a second school board term. Everything I had endured had taken a toll. Many in the community would tell me later that they felt I had abandoned them by not seeking reelection. Many did not know what had transpired behind closed doors during my first four year term. This was because I had been ordered by the FBI not to disclose information relating to their investigation. Much of what I have discussed in this book is the first time I have released the information publicly.

Tom, Ron, and Bill had endured more than I did. I was alone, so I did not have to worry about a family. They all had a wife and children to be concerned with. They all took such a beating from a vicious stronghold that the previous administration had on the district.

They even suffered at the hands of boards members, some of whom supported me. Nadia Davies was elected to replace Ada Reap who lost her bid for reelection.

Nadia appeared to bring strong support to me and my efforts upon her being seated on the board. After a short time, however, she was very difficult to deal with. She had been a teacher within the school district years ago, and had an axe to grind. She had endured a barrage of attacks launched against her by the teacher's union. She faced a heated recall effort due to allegations of her not living within the school district boundaries.

To fight the recall, she was mounting her campaign. However, she began telling Godley and his administration that if they wanted to keep their jobs and continue to enjoy her support, they had better give her financial campaign contributions. She adamantly denied this, however, my trust in Godley told me otherwise. He was a man of strong character, and he and his team would not have lied to me about something like this.

After Godley advised me of her demanding thousands of dollars from him and his cabinet members, I believed her to have committed the crime of extortion. I made the difficult decision to submit the allegations to the FBI, and later to the local District Attorney for their review and possible issuing of criminal charges. When this information came to light, Nadia would turn on Tom Godley and I with a vengeance.

She then threw any ounce of integrity out of the window and arranged a meeting with her once enemy Mike Harrelson. What she then did was unconscionable. Up until this point, the only ones who were aware of the FBI investigation other than me were Tom Godley and possibly some cabinet members who probably witnessed the FBI Agents copying documents on a number of occasions. Because Nadia Davies and her husband Tom had strong knowledge of the finances in the district, I had confided in them in order to obtain information pertinent to the case.

Nadia was then the mastermind of a way to get back at Godley for his not giving into her demands for campaign money, and for his bringing the incident to my attention. Nadia would divulge to Harrelson the fact that the FBI had been conducting an investigation. She gave him specific details as to the scope of the district financial information I had asked of her, which obviously undermined the investigation. In addition, she told Harrelson that she believed on numerous occasions I had worn a body wire placed upon me by the FBI, one such occasion was when Harrelson had offered a bribe to me. She then told Harrelson that she would vote with he and June Mott to terminate Godley which will then allow for Harrelson to stop all additional audits of the district.

To cover his offering a bribe to me, Harrelson immediately contacted the local District Attorney's Office to file a complaint against me for illegally tape recording him. Under California law, it is unlawful to tape record a person without their knowledge. What he did not know was that if the FBI had directed me to wear the wire, I would not be subject to being prosecuted under the California statute.

Harrelson now began contacting Godly and demanding to know what documents the FBI had been privy to and what the specific scope was of their investigation. Harrelson also contacted the district legal counsel Jack Parham demanding to know if he had knowledge of the federal investigation, and wanted to know if Jack could confirm if I had in fact worn a wire and recorded meetings I had with Harrelson. After Harrelson learned of the investigation, I could see the frantic and panic stricken look on his face at future meetings.

In addition, he and June Mott had disclosed to me that they had been in contact with Fred Martinez. We believe they were probably discussing how they could cover their tracks in light of the audits sweeping the district. This was also very interesting that they knew how to contact Fred, as no one else could locate him. In fact, most individuals close to him said that he had fled to Mexico out of fear of being prosecuted. June Mott would later confide in me that she knew that I had been uncovering illegal conduct within the school district, however, she said the people who had committed the wrongdoing were lifelong friends of hers and she felt an obligation to protect them. She implored me to stop the investigation on many occasions.

Just prior to my leaving the board, Nadia Davies in collusion with Harrelson and Mott scheduled a special closed session board meeting to fire Tom Godley. Davies was angry because he did not give in to her attempt to extort money from him and his cabinet members. Harrelson and Mott were now outraged at Godley because he was the driving force of not only insuring that the audits continued, but also the fact that he was closely assisting the FBI with their investigation. Godley was also implementing internal controls to prevent the fraud and mismanagement of funds from occurring again in the future.

I did not know the specific details as to the carefully orchestrated closed session meeting that was about to take place. First and foremost this was in violation of the Brown Act which prohibits elected officials from discussing school business without posting a meeting agenda for the public. In addition to the planned termination of Godley, Nadia had agreed to reinstate a principal at one of the high schools who was close friends with Harrelson and Mott.

During the closed session meeting to which I was presiding as Governing Board President, Harrelson made a motion to reinstate the principal. Mott seconded the motion, and they along with Nadia voted to reinstate the principal while Olson and I voted no. Harrelson then began to make another motion to terminate Tom Godley. Immediately after making the motion, he looked over at Davies, and then halted his motion. He then smiled and said to her, "I believe you were sincere when we talked and what you said, but I can't do this right now." Apparently he felt that this would give the appearance of retaliating against Godley for the FBI investigation.

The next thing I knew, the legal counsel for the district Jack Parham, asked for a break, and requested to speak with me outside of the boardroom. I stepped outside while he and Godley began explaining to me what had transpired. Olson and I had not been fully privy to what exactly had been planned by Davies, Harrelson, and Mott. Parham began to tell me what had happened and that Harrelson had contacted him and told him that Davies told him about the FBI investigation. Parham also confirmed that Harrelson had been told by Davies that I had recorded him during meetings. Harrelson wanted to know how much trouble he could be in. Parham was reluctant to engage with Harrelson in these conversations.

My main concern for the moment was that if Godley were to be terminated, I knew that the board majority of Harrelson, Mott and Davies would appoint an interim superintendent who would thwart the efforts of the investigation. Parham told me that Harrelson agreed not to fire Godley if Godley would agree not to reassign any key staff until after the election to replace Davies.

Just a few months prior to my term expiring, Tom Page was elected to replace Davies. He had been handpicked by the old guard. He was a former CEO for San Diego Gas and Electric. I had hoped that he had integrity and would somehow see the truth.

During a meeting on August 14, 1998, I would see Page stand up to Harrelson. Present at the meeting was, Tom Page, Michael Harrelson, June Mott, Tom Godley, Ron Anderson, Bill Walk, and Marcia was Godley's executive assistant. After discussing items on the agenda, Harrelson asked if everyone could leave the room with the exception of the governing board members.

I then gave Harrelson the floor and asked him what was going on. Harrelson, believing he had Page and Mott with him for a voting block, then made a motion to terminate Godley. Harrelson went on a tirade over the fact that he was angry at Godley for the audits and the FBI investigations. I interrupted Harrelson and advised him that unless Godley had been insubordinate to the board, there was simply no reason to remove him. Page then began siding with me in support of Godley. I was stunned because I knew Godley's adversaries had paid for Page's campaign. Harrelson was dumbfounded. He also became outraged at the audacity of Page to actually be an independent thinker instead of a stooge for Harrelson.

Harrelson began to belittle Page by telling him that he was responsible for Page being elected to public office in the first place. He accused Page of caving in.

I later learned that the FBI had met with Page just after his election to advise him of their conducting an official investigation. I believed that Page learned for the first time that the allegations I had been making were very true. After having heard this directly from the FBI that these allegations were true and very serious had to have been very impacting. Finally, Harrelson accused Page of being a liar. Harrelson said, "You promised us that right after the election you would vote to fire Godley!"

I am not sure who Harrelson thought he was dealing with. Page was a man who had led a billion dollar organization, and Harrelson in his ignorance thought he could play games and intimidate this man? Page started laughing at Harrelson and replied to him, "I have only been in public office for six weeks." Harrelson yelled at Page, "You have had two meetings, two opportunities to fire Godley but you didn't!"

Harrelson then told Page, "My people are not going to allow you to betray them." Page, now getting angry, told Harrelson, "You do not own me! You did not put me in this position!" Page then calmly advised Mott and Harrelson that he needed more time to evaluate the performance of the superintendent and the cabinet members.

I then told Harrelson that he had no credibility with anything he said against Godley because as soon as he was able to confirm the FBI investigation, and that Godley was assisting them in their investigation, Harrelson had done everything in his power to have Godley removed.

Harrelson then made a motion which was seconded by Mott to terminate Godley. Harrelson then leaned over toward Page and said, "Here is the time for you to redeem yourself and support the new board majority by doing what you had promised before the election." Page responded in disgust, "I am not loyal or beholden to anyone". The vote was then taken. Mott and Harrelson voted to fire Godley, and Page and I voted against the motion. Harrelson said to Page, "We are coming after you!" Page then snapped back at Harrelson, "Tell your people to stop putting pressure on me, it is a mathematical formula of resistance; the more you push, the harder I will resist!"

In December 1998, Ted Crooks was elected to the board. He was adamantly opposed to Godley and a staunch supporter of the old guard. Godley left the school district shortly after the election knowing full well that he no longer had the support of the new governing board. This was such a tough time for me. I felt so guilty that I had not run for reelection to support Godley and his team so they could finish the job. I was pretty beat up for a long time.

Perhaps the most frustrating issue with the FBI investigation was the fact that it began to stall. I recall the FBI Special Agent sharing his being very disappointed. He felt that he had sufficiently proved his case; however he said he began receiving pressure from his superiors to back off of the case. When I asked him why he thought this was happening, he told me that politics played into the decisions being made. This was very disheartening.

In addition, I was experiencing personal trials in which I had to examine my own life and my own walk with God. I wrote the following letter to Godley just prior to his leaving.

Dear Tom,

I wanted to encourage you and let you know that I am praying for you more than ever. Do not worry or fret, as the Lord knows what He is doing more than we do. I know you know that, I am just reinforcing it.

Tom, you have been such a strong light to those around you. I have learned more under your leadership in the past 1 ½ years than in my entire life. God has used you so meticulously in the lives of those around you. He has blessed you with a wife to be your pillar as you have embarked on perhaps the roughest ground ever in your life.

The comments I hear from your cabinet members say it all. Your staff sees the strength in your life, and knows it is the Lord! In your weakness you have become so strong Tom, so strong!

I wanted you to have this olive wood hand carving of a shepherd with one of his sheep. This reminded me of how the Lord is carrying you through all this, on His shoulders. This scripture comes to mind:

> *"I am the good shepherd. The good shepherd gives His life for the sheep. "But a hireling, he who is not the shepherd, one who does not own the sheep, sees the wolf coming and leaves the sheep and flees; and the wolf catches the sheep and scatters them. "The hireling flees because he is a hireling and does not care about the sheep. "I am the good shepherd; and I know My sheep, and am known by My own. "As the Father knows Me, even so I know the Father; and I lay down My life for the sheep. "And other sheep I have which are not of this fold; them also I must bring, and they will hear My voice; and there will be one flock and one shepherd. (John 10:11-16 NKJ)*

God has done great things with you Tom, and I will greatly miss having the privilege of watching the intimate details of you leading a ship in such stormy times! Know that I will keep in touch, be praying consistently for you and your cabinet, and never forget the times we have had.

You have helped the Lord mold and make me more than you will ever know. Your sons are so blessed to have you as their Dad! God is with you Tom, and what a sight it is to see you in His arms! One last thought!

Like Shadrach, Meshach, and Abed-Nego, being cast into the burning fiery furnace, you have been as well. Yet Nebuchadnezzar says, "Look!" "I see four men loose, walking in the midst of the fire; and they are not hurt, and the form of the fourth is like the Son of God." That is what is seen here with what you have been through and are going through. The enemies are saying, "Nothing ever happens to this Godley guy, he is still standing!

Forever friends,
Kevin LaChapelle

CHAPTER EIGHT

Circle of Influence

After my time on the school board, and my departure from the police force, I would be in somewhat of a vulnerable state. I would learn very quickly over the years that not all of my friends were really true friends. Friendships would be tested and tried. Many people, whom I thought would help me the most, would actually fail me the most.

I learned that many people had put me on a pedestal, and when I failed them, they were hurt and abandoned our friendship. I would have to really reflect on who I was and what I was about. The next few years of my life would be perhaps more difficult than the previous ten years. I seemed to stay as far away from El Cajon as possible.

I would have such introspection over my life that all of my flaws seemed to magnify themselves over any good that I could ever have done. I had so many flaws, and they became very overwhelming. Fortunately, God gave me a few close friends whom I was able to share all of these burdens with. Instead of abandon me, they shared their flaws as well, and together we began to strengthen ourselves and be accountable to each other.

My being transparent allowed for many other friends including Church Pastors, political leaders, and many others to share with me things, that to be perfectly honest, I wish I had never heard. I was stunned to hear what many of them have never been able to share. This was very similar to how the gang members I would arrest seemed to confide in me. I had a feeling that God was preparing me for a different kind of work.

God seemed to have known I needed time away. I would find myself flying around the country for the next couple of years conducting workshops. This gave me the opportunity to reflect on my life like you cannot even imagine. All of the hours I would spend on planes and in the airports would really cause me to have major introspection. I cannot count the number of total strangers I would meet during my flights, and still keep in touch with many of them today.

I would still get phone calls from San Diego from friends and community members always asking for help. A select few friends would call not for help, but to make sure I was doing okay. They would tell me how much they loved me and that they believed in me always. The people close to me knew I was going through some difficult times. One thing I reflected on more than anything, was the gift God had given me to build relationships with others and the unwavering encouragement I seemed to offer others. People would tell me the impact I had on their life, and it was very humbling.

One such friend was Luis Martinez. I had just ended my stint on the school board and needed a break. I met Luis at Church one Sunday morning through a mutual friend. Luis had been going through a divorce and was trying very hard

to be a good dad for his son. He and I developed a strong friendship almost immediately. Luis was from El Salvador. I would later take two different trips with him to El Salvador to spend time with his family. Luis is now remarried, has another son, and one on the way. He exemplifies what it is to be the protector for his family. As soon as the lights came on in Luis' mind, and he knew what he needed to do to be a strong leader, he jumped on it. He immediately began helping his family and sharing with his brothers what it meant to be a real man. He would teach them that a man is to be the protector and stand up for the weak and resist the negative destructive behaviors that take so many young people hostage. Luis is a pillar for many in his circle of influence.

Over and over I get asked how I am able to have such an impact on those around me. What is your secret, some ask? Much of what I have learned over the years I will attempt to explain and share. First of all, you must

ask yourself a question. Why try to influence or impact those around you? I mean after all, no one ever tries to influence you, or do they? We all have the opportunity to influence others and likewise be influenced ourselves. The big

issue is this: Are you an influencer, or just a person who is influenced? The other issue is this; do you seek people who have something to offer to you, or do you seek out people and wonder what you may offer to them? I chose to see people and dream about their potential to have an impact in this world. The other principal I never forget is this; to have good friends, you must first be a good friend!

You may feel that you really do not have that much influence on others, or the fact that others may not necessarily have much influence over you. Consider this: How much does it cost to air a thirty second commercial, especially during a Super Bowl game? Why? Advertisers know how easily people can be influenced, and how that influence drives sales. If they are willing to spend as much money as they do for a thirty second slot of influence, imagine what you can do for others by being a positive influence in their life.

Who is in your circle of influence? This term applies to the concept that every person has a "circle" of people around them that they interact with on a regular basis, and whose decisions they can influence. These people include spouses and family, co-workers and friends. The ability for an individual in this circle to affect the decisions made by the others is very strong. Some people surround themselves with yes people. They want everyone around them to agree with everything they say or do. I on the other hand, chose to surround myself with people who are not afraid to challenge me and my beliefs. I have a saying in my office that goes like this: If the both of us agree on everything, one of us needs to go! Iron sharpens iron.

It is also important to share your dreams and vision with those in your circle. You need to become a part of each others lives. Jesus said it is better to give than to receive. This truth has blessed my life more than ever. I am blessed with some of the most incredible friendships ever.

You have to overcome the insecurity of demanding a return for your investment in others on your own terms. For example influencing others can be easily abused. Pyramid schemes are a perfect example. You know the type. You receive a call from that friend of yours you have not heard from in a while. They invite you over for dinner, and oh yes, they do want to discuss something very special with you. They go on to tell how they have found an incredible opportunity and want to share it with only a few of their most special friends. They are just trying to suck you in. They might also say, "I am so excited as to what I stumbled upon, and I want you to be a part of it too!" When you arrive, they begin to share with you about their newfound wealth. This is incredibly manipulative. If you abuse friendships like this, you will not only lose friends, they will despise you. Anytime you hear dollar signs, you better wake up and open your eyes. Anyone trying to influence others for self gain will become evident and your true motives will be clear to others.

If you want others to open up to you, you had better be ready to open up to them. People tend to only make themselves vulnerable to those who have made themselves vulnerable as well. For some people this is very difficult. You must take the risk. This is why it is so important for you to determine who you should influence. When you develop a solid support system around you, you will know when it is the right time to open up and share with those around you. Don't forget, to have good friends, you must first be a good friend. If you ever breach that trust, you are doomed for failure in relationships.

After having developed a close relationship with God and sensing a calling in my life to lead others around me, I began to see clearly how much friends can impact each other. I did not feel a calling to lead others as most people define leading, but that God would use me to seek out the people in this world that others may see as failures. I always prayed I would be used to motivate them and develop them into becoming strong leaders with character. They would end up being God driven, and be able to resist and deflect tremendous pressure and negative influence from others. That is the purpose God has given to me! I help them prepare themselves to have an enormous impact on this world. If we are not having an impact, than we are irrelevant. Most people desire relevance and purpose in life.

Recently, I was talking to a friend who was having problems with his marriage. He has four young children as well. He felt helpless and purposeless in his life. I told him how men have forgotten what it means to be a strong man. For example, a husband and father must take seriously their role. In their family, they had better bring adventure and purpose to their family. A woman wants a man who will lead with purpose and bring excitement to the family. Likewise, kids love excitement and adventure. If the man does not provide this within the family, then their kids will search for it somewhere else. They may find the excitement in street gangs. If you cannot provide this for your wife, she will find the excitement she longs for with or without you.

A man must have the wisdom to rally the family together for a unified purpose. Whether it is outdoor adventures, helping build homes in Mexico or whatever, the family will thrive on this. Anyone that knows me knows that I always have something going on and it is always full of excitement and adventure. I do not even have to try. God seems to just open the doors and I choose to walk through them. This friend of mine told me, "This sounds like too much work." It may be, but what is the alternative, a family full of chaos?

I remember when I performed the marriage ceremony for my brother. After giving a short talk about the role of the family, I was stunned at how many people approached me after the ceremony. They told me of their marriage being on the brink of failure. They told me of all the things they felt they had done wrong. When I told them it was never too late to change, they seemed to find a ray of hope. We seem to forget that tomor-  row is the first day of the rest of our life. Sure we may have consequences from our past inadequacies; however you would be surprised at how resilient people are. We can never take relationships for granted, as they are the cement for our lives.

Mentoring Relationships

Over the years one of my main missions has been to mentor and send individuals into law enforcement armed with the ability to resist the negative subcultures within law enforcement. I had been very careful to advise these individuals to make sure that they do not put my name on their application as a reference. The reason is because many in the law enforcement circle do not appreciate who I am or what I stand for.

An example of what can happen to a police recruit candidate is this: This recruit had applied for a local police department. Unfortunately he had put my name down as a reference on his application. When he was interviewed for his background, the investigator appeared stunned to see my name on the application. The officer asked him how he knew of me, and then told him in a sarcastic tone, "Tell Kevin we said hello." Consequently he was never called back for consideration. Because most agencies do not seem to have an appreciation for whistle blowers, I have learned to send guys in stealth mode.

Officers must be very careful in this profession. Most of what I have taught individuals seeking a career in the policing field is that the temptations are so great, that they must put controls in place in their lives both personally and professionally to resist such behavior. An example of what can happen if you do not put controls in place, happened to a San Diego Police Officer.

I became acquainted with him and his wife years ago. On one occasion, when I saw this officer, he gave me his business card which contained his personal cellular phone number on it. I immediately questioned him and asked him if he knew the possible consequences for putting this number on his card for the public. He laughed at me telling me how I get carried away with my position on ethical standards. I then explained to him that he will be responding to calls for service and will appear as a knight in shining armor for many individuals including females. I told him that if they ever asked him for his card, and he gave it to them, he was opening the door for trouble. I lectured him regarding one of the greatest flaws in today's law enforcement circles which are sexual immorality. Again, he did not take me seriously.

I tried to explain how important it is to make your convictions known to others around you. Others will size you up to see what you are all about. Misery loves company. Other guys would love to see you compromise your values so that they can rationalize their destructive behavior. I told him of a story in which I was walking, going to eat lunch with an officer from SDPD. He did not know me that well, nor did I know him that well. As we were walking into the restaurant, he saw a pretty woman. He said to me, "Wouldn't you love to $%#& her!" Instead of ignoring it, I chose to confront him about it. I immediately asked him, "I thought you were married?" He told me he was but that did not mean he could not look. I began to share with him how disappointed I was with what he had said. Weeks went by, and he called me one day. He called to thank me for confronting him on his comments. He told me that no one had ever done that before, and it made him really think about who he was and what he stood for. After telling this story to my friend, he did not seem too impressed with the lesson.

I had not seen this officer for quite a while. One day, I received a phone call from his wife crying. She told me that he was having an affair with a girl he met on duty. She was devastated. I called him, and he was crying as well. He asked if I would go meet with him in which I did. He cried pretty hard acknowledging that what he had done was very destructive to his wife and child. He asked me if I would help him get back up. Of course I agreed.

During my counseling with the both of them, an issue came up where he did not want his wife having access to his cell phone bills nor his voice mail password. I told them that transparency was essential in regaining the trust that had been lost. I told him, if he was still having secrets, than he was not genuinely remorseful, and told her he was probably still cheating. A few months later, she called me crying again. She told me that the affair had never stopped. I explained to her that is why I told them they must have transparency and no secrets to be successful in their marriage.

The officer then called me telling me he was in trouble with internal affairs for running the license plates of females. I asked him if he did so, and he tried to rationalize it. I then told him, his best option was to resign from the police department because he clearly could not handle the commitment, nor could he resist the temptations. He agreed, but then cut me out of his life and remained an officer for quite a while.

Months and months went by, and then I received a call from his wife telling me that while he was off duty in a bar with one of his flings, he was involved in a domestic dispute and the police were called and arrested him. Again, he was remorseful for maybe a week or two. I told his wife that she must wake up and protect herself and her child from this nonsense. I told her that I did not believe that he would change. I told him the same thing. I told him he was a disgrace to his badge. He was placed on telephone report duty and eventually settled the case and was put back out on patrol. His wife finally did seek a divorce, which was granted.

Finally, several more months went by, and I received another call from his wife telling me that they were trying to reconcile their marriage even after divorce. I told her to be very careful as I saw him as being very manipulative. A few more months went by, and she called to tell me that he was drunk, came into her home and forced himself on her sexually. He was ripping her clothes off when their child walked in, and he ordered the child into a closet and continued raping his ex-wife. The police came, he was arrested, and this time finally forced to resign his position as a police officer.

Unfortunately, the number of calls I receive with regards to infidelity within the ranks of police officers is staggering. One thing I must always remember is that I have been called to see people's weaknesses and then help them overcome them. Many see a person's flaws and exploit them and use it to destroy them. For example a verse found in Genesis 50:20 says, "And as for you, you meant evil against me, {but} God meant it for good in order to bring about this present result." What is important is that when we make a mistake, we put the necessary controls in our life to prevent it from occurring again.

It is imperative that anyone choosing a career in law enforcement understand the necessary commitments one must possess. This profession is very unique. If you are seeking a position with pre-eminence or status, this job is not for you. Unless you are principally driven to be a light in your community, and have a servanthood style of leadership, you will fail and be more of a detriment to the badge.

To be an effective police officer, you must first have strong character. There must be something outside of yourself that you are being held to a higher standard. For me, it was my personal relationship with God. This personal relationship was above everything else. A higher calling, if you will. If you are not convinced that there is a higher calling for your being a police officer, you will encounter serious problems. It is not about what you can get out of being a police officer. It is about how you can be used to empower others in your community. You have a tremendous opportunity to touch the lives of multitudes in your capacity as a police officer. Or you have the potential of undermining the very people and communities to which you serve by abdicating your role and responsibility.

CHAPTER NINE

A New Challenge

I knew that God had allowed me to experience all I had been through for a reason. I wanted to put the experience I had gained to good use fighting corruption in communities and in other police departments where officers might find themselves in situations similar to mine in El Cajon. What I had been through had been painful, but I had learned a lot from the experience and believed strongly that I might be able to help other men and women who wanted to become police officers, helping them learn what to watch for and how to handle the moral crises that might come. I also wanted to find some way to assist communities in dealing with scams and fraud and in dealing with officials who were derelict in their duty in office.

Special Investigations Agency

In 1999, even while still traveling around the country, I formed the Special Investigations Agency (SIA). At first, it was just me and an idea, but I soon began forming a network of volunteers inside law enforcement and outside, who are dedicated to the same ideals that all law enforcement officers are supposed to have: "To Protect and To Serve." For me, those words have never been just a mere slogan. They are a commitment to do everything in my power to ensure that a community is protected and served by its local law enforcement agency.

Then, too, there are many problems that, however dedicated police officers are, they do not always have time to investigate due to required urgent action involving violent crimes. I knew that the problems I found when serving as a Trustee in the Grossmont Union School District were occurring elsewhere. Being a public official entails being in a position of trust for the community—acting on their behalf and in their interest. For some people, even if they would not be disposed to criminal behavior under other circumstances, the power and control over funds that they have as public officials become too great a temptation to resist. And the citizens of the community are often unaware of or feel unable to do anything to stop the abuse of power and remove the officials.

I wanted to help citizens everywhere become empowered to deal with issues affecting their cities, and the network of volunteers I began recruiting had the same commitment, at first in our area, then throughout California, and finally across the nation.

A good deal of our work at SIA focuses on those people in communities who are most vulnerable to being the victims of scams, fraud, and misrepresentation. Immigrants, the elderly, the poor, and the sick—all are ready prey for scam artists who see an easy buck to be made out of someone else's misery or ignorance. Even more, we are finding and stopping corruption in our elected officials and in the way they manage our cities. Often times I receive calls from elected or appointed officials asking how they can try and expose governmental corruption within their own ranks. They generally want me to do the dirty work, so they will not in any way have to face the controversy. I also receive many calls from police officers facing decisions after they see corruption within their department. They all say the same thing! Please don't tell anyone I called you. If they know I am connected to you, they will come after me.

One example would be when I received a call from a former officer from El Cajon. I did not know him as he was not an officer during my time there. He had heard of me and wanted to share things that he had seen in the department that he knew were wrong. I told him my story and what he was up against. I never heard back from him, but I did learn that they ran him out of the department a short time later.

Another officer called me to tell me how the department began to retaliate against him for his questioning of their unethical activities. How did they go after him? Unbelievable! His wife worked for the Grossmont School District. One day, an FBI Agent arrived at her work and detained her telling her that her husband had been arrested for serious crimes. Simultaneously, her husband, the El Cajon Officer, had been arrested by the FBI and transported to the El Cajon Police Station. They began to interrogate him on allegations of laundering money. He was stunned. The end result was that they had to apologize to him and drop all charges because the allegations were baseless. After he sued, he learned that the FBI had been acting on a tip from guess who? You guessed it, Lt. "S"! His case is still pending. Last I heard they were trying to reach a settlement with him. He is no longer with the department.

I do all I can to give good guidance when I receive calls from officers from different agencies. Many know of my experience, others do research and come across our SIA website. After reading my story, they call for support. I enjoy being a support for them, as I wished I had the same support when I went through my experience.

SIA Investigations: Case Histories

The Case of Underreported Crime

How does a Police Department reduce its crime rate? Simple—just don't report all the crimes committed. In 2005, S.I.A. began one of the biggest investigations since its founding. We received reports from citizens that the San Diego Police Department has been able to show a reduction in crime by refusing to file reports by citizens who are victims of a crime. Similarly, when retail establishment's place shoplifters under a citizen's arrest, the police refuse to process the suspect and do not file an arrest report. Instead, they merely file a "Field Interview" card. However, the victim in both cases is led to believe erroneously that an arrest report has been completed. Sometimes the police officer would outright refuse to complete a report. In other cases, the victim has been threatened with being arrested himself/herself unless he dismisses the citizen's arrest he has made against another. After obtaining a wealth of statistics, we found that the San Diego Police Department only completed a case report in 8% of the calls for service, whereas the San Diego Sheriff's Department filed reports in 23% of the cases, and the Los Angeles Police Department, filed 21% of the cases. Officers within the San Diego Police Department state that they have been directed to show a high number of radio calls to which they responded but low crime statistics. By filling out only a Field Interview card instead of an arrest report or crime report, the incidence of crime reported is artificially low. When retail store managers have reported shoplifters, they are told the police are no longer required to issue citations when the managers make a citizen's arrest.

The California Penal Code recently was amended to allow officers discretion in processing a citizen's arrest. As a result, the police are losing any accountability for not reporting crimes. The intent of the Amendment was quite different; it was meant to allow officers not to take into custody any person when he had not committed a crime even though a citizen's arrest had been made.

Recently, a college student who was mentoring young people to help them resist gang influence called the police after witnessing older gang members forcing young kids to fight. He had intervened and was attacked by a gang member. The police officer investigating the incident told the gang member that he could avoid a citizen's arrest by threatening to arrest the mentor. Of course he agreed.

In another incident, a 12-year old boy was walking home from his school when he was confronted by several older youths who held a knife to his throat and demanded his bicycle and his money. The boy's older brother called the police, and the officer told the boy's family that there was nothing they could do.

We have received reports of a number of sexual assaults in the Mission Valley area of San Diego. One woman reported to us that several months ago, she was pulled into the river bed while walking from the Trolley Station. Fortunately, she was able to fight off the attacker and she escaped to safety. After calling police, she said they arrived over two hours later and told her that because two hours had gone by after her attack, there was really nothing that could be done. The police officers who answered her call did not complete a police report. When I showed her a police sketch of one of the recent suspects, she believed it may have been her attacker as well. Had the police been proactive and handled the first assault properly, the recent attacks may have been prevented.

This is not an isolated case. We have been finding that all across the U.S. many police departments over the past few years have been exposed through audits that they have been underreporting crime to give a better perception of their city for tourism. For example, the Atlanta, Georgia, Police Department was underreporting crime before, during, and long after the 1996 Summer Olympics. When a new chief of police, Richard Pennington, was appointed in 2002, he reported that the police department had been underreporting crime to enhance its image as a tourist destination. The Department had discarded crime records and improperly closed cases. Pennington said that the department was "broken" and needed 500 more police officers to operate effectively, adding that the current low starting salary has caused many good officers to leave the Department for better-paying jobs. The report has come as a shock to Atlanta's citizens who believed that traffic was a bigger problem than crime. Pennington came to Atlanta from New Orleans, where during his tenure numerous cases were solved and crime actually did decrease significantly, and he is working hard to turn around the Police Department in Atlanta now.

In Chicago we have also found some disturbing trends. Let us examine statistical data from Chicago, Illinois. The following statistical information was obtained from the Chicago Police Departments 2004 Annual Report. The population statistics were obtained from the State of Illinois.

The first graph shows a trend with an increase in population. The second graph shows an increased trend for 911 calls for service for the City of Chicago. The cause for an increase in calls for service typically coincides with population growth. The third and final graph shows a decreased trend in total crimes for the City of Chicago.

Is crime really down? How is this possible? With an increase in population and calls for service, could crime be decreasing? Or, could it be that officers are discouraged from taking crime reports to show a façade of a decrease in crime.

We believe that San Diego, Atlanta, and numerous other cities across the country all have significantly underreported crime. A low crime rate in a big city encourages tourism, which can bring a big economic boost to a community. But when the crime rate is actually underreported, the long-term reputation of those cities is in jeopardy. One theory some chief's of police subscribe to is that if you give a perception of a decrease in crime to a community, than the crime may actually decrease based solely on this false perception. Can you imagine that?

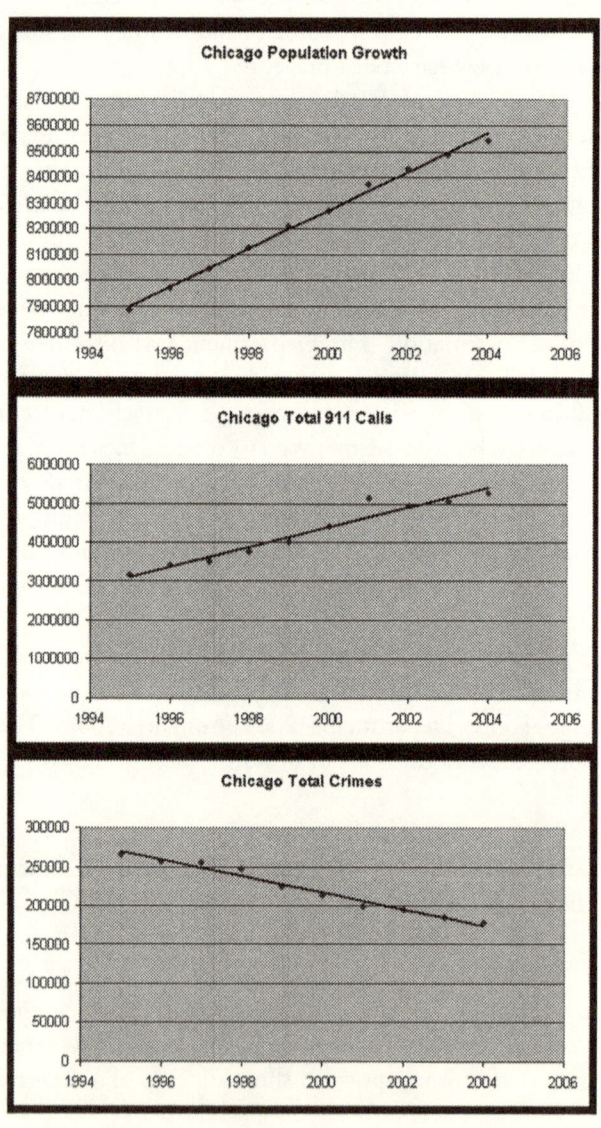

After our story aired on Channel Ten news as their top story, I began receiving phone calls. I knew the fight was on. San Diego Police Chief William Lansdowne was obviously not happy with our allegations against him and his department. I began hearing from police officers that my assertions were correct however they could not jeopardize their career by coming forward. I prayed, "God, please help us find at least one officer willing to come forward. I met with many officers, but all insisted they would not consent to a video interview even if we hid their identity.

Finally, a friend of a friend told me of an officer that they believed had character and would talk to me. I made a cold call to the officer which was somewhat awkward as I did not know what the officer's response would be. Often times when people hear the name LaChapelle, they cringe knowing I usually call when I am investigating something. I called the officer and said, "Hi, this is Kevin LaChapelle, I wanted to see if you would be willing to talk with me." I was waiting for the officer to hang up the phone, but to my surprise, the officer said, "Sure, go ahead." We talked for a while about my allegations to which the officer acknowledged that this was in fact happening. I asked the officer if we could meet somewhere to talk further and the officer agreed. The officer wanted to meet far away so the officer would not be seen with me. We set the place, date, and time. I was waiting for a cancellation call, but never received one.

On the date and time we set, I drove to the location, and waited in front of the location. A few minutes went by, and there the officer was. The officer said, "Kevin?" I said yes, and we began talking. The officer shared with me the fact that the San Diego Police Department is so understaffed, and that the morale was so incredibly low. The officer shared how disgusted they are with their current Chief of Police William Lansdowne. The officer said that Lansdowne had been cooking the books in a number of ways. The officer acknowledged our assertion that Lansdowne had been methodically underreporting crime to show an artificial decrease in crime. The officer also explained how Lansdowne had directed officers not to check the box on crime reports that distinguishes the crime as gang related. Specifically, unless there was gang on gang violence, officers where told not to check the box. For example, if there was a carjacking and the suspect was a gang member, but the victim was just an ordinary citizen, the officers were told to consider the crime as not gang related. This was an effort to show a decrease in gang crimes. The officer also told of a memo that was recently circulated in which the prioritizing of calls was changed in order to artificially decrease the response times.

I had to come to a point in which I would ask the officer to agree to a video taped interview in which we would hide his identity and change the officer's voice. Finally, the officer said sternly, "OK, I will do it!" The officer went on to say that the department needed to get this out in the open so the public would know the real condition of crime in the city.

The next week Channel Ten News aired a follow-up story in which the officer's video interview would be released. We are demanding Chief William Lansdowne's resignation because we do not foresee that he will be honest with the public and the city counsel.

The Case of the Immigrant ID Cards

Almost anywhere you go these days, whether you're writing a check, obtaining a driver's license, or even getting a library card, you are asked to show two forms of identification, one of which must have your photo. New immigrants often lack a driver's license or any form of picture ID, even if they have a Social Security card. This makes them ripe targets for scam artists, and we found one such group in San Diego, California, who offer to sell poor immigrants a "legal" ID card at an outrageous price.

Calle & Associates advertises itself as the only company registered in the U.S. to sell these so-called "legal" ID cards. We sent in SIA Investigator Jose Orozco with an undercover camera to investigate Calle & Associates' operations. Our camera captured on video a sales presentation by a Calle & Associates' employee, who told Orozco that the cards come with a seal and a "legal identification card number." The identification number on the card has no validity and cannot be tracked through the state and federal system databases, making it worthless for any legal identification purpose—and the official "seal" is nothing more than an imprint of the state flag of California.

The price for these so-called ID cards showed clearly that Calle & Associates' operation constituted a scam. Orozco was told he would have to pay $400 up front, and then make two additional payments of $200 each for the card. That's $800 for a card that's not worth the paper it's printed on! In the U.S., there's no such thing as an ID card issued under approval of the U.S. government, and states issue picture ID cards to non-drivers for a small fee. In fact, according to the California Department of Motor Vehicles, a visitor in this country can use his home country's driver's license as identification—he doesn't even have to get an international driver's license. California law makes it illegal for a private company to sell any ID similar in size and form to one offered by the State of California, who routinely issues ID cards to California residents who need a picture ID but who do not drive. Uncovering scams such as this one and bringing them to the attention of the new media and law enforcement agencies is a primary function of SIA.

San Diego's National City Councilman Soto Told To Resign by SIA!

Beleaguered Councilman Fred Soto was asked to step down from office amidst mounting complaints from his former law office clients that he took their monies without rendering legal service.

At a session of the city council of National City on Tuesday, Nov. 14, 2000, Nenita Rosales, a leader of a Filipino group, filed a petition signed by at least 35 residents demanding that Soto quit his position as councilman, the post he won in the 1998 election. "We find that he (Soto) is an embarrassment to our city and his actions are not commensurable to those of a city council member," the petition stated.

The Special Investigations Agency, a watchdog group advocating for clean government, also asked Soto to resign, and for the city government to find legal sanctions that may be imposed on Soto. "Soto is a disgrace upon his position as a city council member. And his acts are a real shame," said Kevin LaChapelle, director of the SIA, during the city council session. All throughout the proceedings, Soto slumped quietly in his seat. He never said a word to defend himself, nor at least tried to.

The only time Soto spoke was when he delivered an invocation that preceded the session but even then, LaChapelle thought it was odd that Soto did it. "I have a really difficult time with you doing the invocation," he stated, addressing Soto when the time came for the public to speak. But Councilman Ralph Inzunza, who was seating next to Soto, took the cudgels for him. At one point he tried to stop LaChapelle from speaking. LaChapelle insisted he had been given five minutes to talk to the city council. Mayor Waters, who presided over the session, agreed, saying whether LaChapelle said embarrassing things or not, he had his five minutes. Inzunza yielded. After LaChapelle's brief but strong remarks, Inzunza took the floor and explained that the cases against Soto should be taken to the court. He said it was wrong to bring out the cases, which he considered private, during a council meeting when officials are discussing the business of the city. Soto ultimately resigned his counsel position. Soto has surrendered his license to practice law following complaints field against him to the State Bar of California. The California Supreme Court accepted his resignation on Oct. 14, 2000, "with charges pending".

The Case of the "Healing" Cards

If ever a group was vulnerable to being enticed to part with their money, it's those who are desperately ill and seek a cure—grasping at the proverbial straw to find some help for their illness. SIA found the Gentle Wind Project, a company headquartered in Maine, who sells cards that Gentle Wind claims that these "healing instruments" are "based on technology from the spirit world" and offers them for "donations" in upwards of thousands of dollars to the public! SIA was contacted by nearly four dozen people from across the United States and the United Kingdom reporting that Gentle Wind Project, sometimes calling itself "Eye of the Sky," has bilked desperate people out of thousands of dollars all in the name of "helping others."

This group holds seminars across the country asserting that they have the only healing instrument technology. As a result, SIA has managed to garner major news coverage alerting the public to their operations and is cooperating with the State Attorney in Maine to investigate this scam.

The Case of a Missing San Diego Businessman

In 1996 SIA received a call from a woman, Leigh Hughes advising us of a situation in which a Christian family could not find their husband and father. Each year the dad would take a trip to the Sierras to meditate on his business plans and he failed to return. The family complained that the San Diego Police Department refused to listen to them telling the wife that he probably had left her for another woman. The family knew that this could not be true.

I agreed to help on behalf of S.I.A. our non profit organization. I immediately found that none of his credit cards had been used and his bank accounts were untouched. I told the wife, I felt he may have been involved in an accident in which his vehicle may have left the roadway. We began amassing a search of where he usually would go to. Viet Hollenberg and her son Aaron would be so strong in this devastating time. Their husband and father Russell was missing. Unknown to us, the police had not entered his vehicle into the computer system so that if another law enforcement agency ran the license plate it would show that it was tied to a missing person case. Russell's vehicle was found by game wardens in the Sierra Mountains, but had no idea that he was missing. Finally, we learned of his vehicles location and headed to that area to start our search.

We arrived armed with volunteers and began our trek up the mountainous area. Russell's son Aaron came with us. I would learn very quickly that this 18 year old young man was solid as a rock in his life. We searched for several days. This was a rough area. Finally the only area left to search was very difficult terrain and we opted to charter a helicopter. Leigh Hughes raised the funds to pay for the helicopter. We needed a jet helicopter due to the altitude and terrain. This was about $500.00 an hour. A friend of mine, Steve Morales, and I met the helicopter and coordinated with our team members on the ground with via radio contact. It did not take long. Steve and I could see a colored piece of clothing. We circled the area and advised our ground units what we had seen. They threw down the rope and began to rappel to where we could see something. My friend David Rios was the first on the scene. I yelled on the radio, "Do not allow Aaron to go down," as I did not want him to see his father in this condition.

David Rios radioed back to us that he was near the clothing, and confirmed a body was in fact found. He appeared to have been deceased for some time. It appeared that he had slipped down a ravine and was unable to climb back out due to the icy conditions. I remember Aaron running down to see his Dad. I could see him from the helicopter. I wanted to jump out and grab him, but it was too late.

Steve and I landed at a nearby air field and made our way back to the area where Mr. Hollenberg had been found. I looked at Aaron; he shed tears as did I. He was so strong about it. He was happy to have been able to be there and bring closure for his mother and his younger sister. Aaron and I developed a very strong relationship over the years and to this day keep in touch. He has since graduated from University of San Diego and is a brilliant businessman.

County Prosecutor Seeking Support

In October 2005, we received a call from a county prosecutor in Texas. This woman began to share how her house had been burned to the ground and how she had been subject to major harassment for seeking justice against a corrupt judge. Preliminarily I was reluctant to believe her story. However, while I was talking with her on the phone I was asking her pertinent information about who was involved in this corruption case. As she told me names, I began researching them on the internet as we spoke. I was stunned to see newspaper articles regarding what she was telling me. Most people do not want to believe this type of corruption still exists today. This woman was so courageous! She stood up for what she knew was right. She sacrificed her family, home, safety, and reputation. The FBI was on the verge of issuing an indictment against the judge, and a few days later the judge killed himself. There were many others implicated in this corruption scandal. However, according to the prosecutor, the FBI backed off after of the case. It is sad that the FBI sometimes appears today more as a political body instead of a law enforcement body. We will do all we can to support this courageous prosecutor!

Fulfilling Our Mission

SIA continues to grow in strength and presence across the U.S., thanks to the volunteers from all walks of life who have joined us in helping to stop fraud and find answers to problems such as that of the missing San Diego man. Our goal is to ensure that every community becomes empowered to take action to protect its citizens against corruption and apathy wherever it may occur. Our mission statement sums up our values and commitment:

> To educate, promote, and assure integrity and ethics by providing
> an investigative and intervention resource to the general public.

We have instituted training for organizations in areas such as gang intervention, workplace violence prevention, theft prevention, and fraud prevention. We continue to work with citizens who come to us as individuals and organizations who seek our assistance. Recently, our outreach has included Mexico as well as the U.S., where we are working with a courageous police officer across the border who is seeking to stop corruption among the police and public officials in his town. SIA cannot be everywhere, but our volunteers can be in each community, be it large or small and SIA will serve as a nexus for their efforts to provide safe cities and towns everywhere across America. But to do this we must continue to grow our base of volunteers to make this vision of SIA a reality.

I am fortunate to have the opportunity to teach college classes at some local colleges. The subject matter that I teach is law enforcement operations, community policing, and law enforcement ethics. As you can imagine from the subjects, this is an incredible opportunity to mentor college students and help them understand how important it is to take a stand. I am amazed at many of the stories I hear from my students with regards to experiences either they, or someone they know have had with law enforcement. I hope they never forget those stories as most of them have ultimate goals of joining law enforcement as a career. Hopefully they will never become what had given them a bad taste as to what being a police officer is all about.

CHAPTER TEN

My Heroes

Here are the guys who never cease to amaze me. I am so blessed at what they have become with their lives. They stand for what they believe, and they try to help those around them. These guys are heroes to me because of what they have conquered in their lives. They are solid, and have been able to take their eyes off of themselves and put them on others. I will share a little on each of these incredible friends. Then, they will share our story. When you read about how God touched these lives, I hope you ponder how much God wants to use you to touch those around you.

Jeff Cramer was at my side through tumultuous times. It is amazing how much God knew how much I would need someone in my life that only Jeff could have provided. Here is Jeff's account of our story:

> *I can remember just as if it were yesterday, a typical hot summer afternoon in El Cajon, California. The temperature had to be 100 degrees or more. However, this particular afternoon at age 19, I would meet the Police Officer that would be instrumental in changing the rest of my life. This was the day I met El Cajon Police Officer Kevin LaChapelle.*
>
> *The scene was in front of a liquor store in about the five hundred block of Broadway. My brother Chris had confronted a clerk that had short-changed my soon to be wife and mother and it evolved into a public disturbance. The police were called.*
>
> *I showed up just as the police had arrived and attempted to make my way over to my brother, who was still yelling at the clerk. It was here that Officer LaChapelle stepped in front of me and stopped me. This short stocky little man gave me a stern, but professional warning, which I neglected to follow. Who was this little guy? He was not going to stop me! Doesn't he know that this is my little brother needing help? To my surprise, Officer LaChapelle pulled out his PR-24 police baton faster than I cold even process his command. The situation was serious and he was not taking any chances. I rapidly saw it his way and sat down on the curb.*

It could not have been more than a year later and I found myself in the back halls of the El Cajon Police Department. This time it was as a uniformed Reserve Cadet. I had just started the reserve phase of the police academy and the El Cajon Police Department was my sponsor. This was my first time in uniform at the department, and who do you think I ran into? Oh yes, that stocky little cop that had a way of helping me see the light just a year earlier. I am not a fearful guy by nature, but I panicked and tried to avoid this dude. He saw me, but did not recognize me.

The weeks went by and I could not avoid him any longer. Officer LaChapelle was assigned as my training officer by the 3rd watch Sergeant. MAN! How could this happen? God must hate me!

I watched and learned from Kevin and saw that this guy was the real deal; he was a super cop; if there was a crime, if there was something wrong, he was there. My respect and trust in him grew week-after-week. Then during one shift I found myself confessing to Kevin about the event that had occurred a year and half earlier and reminded him of the first time we had actually met. He laughed and commented at how ironic the situation was. He told me that God must have a great plan for me, little did I know, he was right—again!

Kevin had a knack at working with the youth and was known for his street connections amongst the gangs. He took the time for community policing and knew what was happening in his patrol area. Kevin believed in young people no matter what walk of life they came from. Kevin continued to excel as a cop and was awarded numerous awards time and time again for his excellence as an officer.

Simultaneously, he was also growing in his compassion for helping the youth. Kevin was the kind of cop that would arrest you as a gang member on Saturday, but would take the time to visit you and encourage you off-duty as a Volunteer-In-Probation. What, a cop that arrests you and then visits you in jail to help you get your life back on track. That's right he has a genuine love in helping others. Kevin did not just use the often air-filled words of, "I really want to help people," as a tactic to get hired as a police officer. Kevin used these words because it was a way of life that he believed in from his heart.

Kevin believed so heavily in troubled youth that he rallied community members together and opened a youth center right in the toughest part of El Cajon. His efforts helped to create a positive environment for the troubled youth. His compassion and commitment to the community through the youth was growing and the news media began to take notice. He was the focus of television interviews and the recipient of multiple community leadership awards.

Well it was about this time that a few officers who had a different view of troubled youth began to give Kevin a hard time about his off-duty work and his faith in God. They did not have the same sympathetic feelings and altruistic view towards struggling people. Anyway, the struggle began as the popularity and award-laced reputation of Kevin grew. He became a righteous hero amongst the troubled youth and their families. Yet amongst the brotherhood behind the badge, he was losing popularity. Kevin had excelled up the police ranks over the last 5-7 years and was now reporting directly to the Police Chief for his assignments and direction. Rank and file officers did not like this nor did certain field supervisors. Why? Did the department not receive good accolades and a growing favor from among the community? Yes of course, but there are certain unwritten procedures you follow in the trenches. Chiefly, you do not help the people you arrest!

Time went on and Kevin's freedom grew and the glow of his badge reached an all-time high with city officials, police administration, and the community.

The School Liaison Program was the new focus of Kevin's police work. Kevin began to operate at the local high schools within the Grossmont School District and again his popularity grew. He ran for and was elected as a Public Official on the Board of Trustees for the Grossmont School District. Wow! By trade a Police Officer; by volunteer an Elected Board Member and Public Official.

Then it happened—the proverbial gauntlet—Kevin was approached by someone who had information to give him regarding a crime that would top the "Internal Investigations Black List." An officer had raped a 15-year old girl. Think about this with me for a moment: What are the chances of this happening? A cop that has become a community hero for helping troubled youth; a cop who has become a refuge for the lost and hurting; a cop that has won numerous awards and has become influential amongst police officials, city officials, and community leaders; a cop that is beginning to face animosity amongst a strange growing number of fellow cops as he acts on the report of a rape on a female youth. "Please God, Don't Let My Badge Tarnish!"

Kevin did what he was sworn to do. He protected and served the community he was committed to, even though it would ultimately cost him everything.

A report was taken and charges were filed against the fellow officer. This would be one of the hardest days of his sworn life. As the case grew and the details from the investigation began to come forth, the picture was clear, not only was it a fellow officer, it was also discovered that Kevin's lieutenant's adult son was also a perpetrator in this heinous crime with a second victim. It is no wonder that a small amount of officers opposed Kevin. They had seen what appeared to be a super-cop success over the last several years and probably had an uneasy fear of exposure.

Implausible as it may seem, this battle and the ones to follow became a battle between light and dark. Kevin rested heavily on God and took strength in the friendships of those around him. Yet the question rang on, "God how could this be? Say it is not so." Kevin had poured his heart and soul into performing his duty as a Police Officer and God had developed it into a life saving operation for so many of us, both as youth and adults.

It was a difficult time for Kevin and he wrestled with his feeling a sense of alienation from fellow officers. Many of them agreed with him, but did not have the courage to fight the battle alongside of him. Secretly, officers would encourage him; high-ranking members of the police administration would leak plans from others directed against Kevin and even would warn him of plots to destroy his reputation, or even take his life. Yes I said, "Take his life."

It was his life's dream to be a police officer, but now he was beginning to see signs of a tarnishing badge. As the shield was growing dull it appeared that Kevin was seeing a new vision and was being prepared for a new battle. Time came and went and Kevin got the victory over the corruption and was left unscathed. Nonetheless, somehow he grew. The mental tenacity he had acquired as a cop prepared him for the emerging call into a higher level of investigation. You see, as I mentioned earlier, Kevin was promoted to a much higher level of authority. As an elected official he had been assigned by the public to confront the scandalous financial and policy corruption of the Grossmont Union High School District. The general public had faith in him; no they loved him.

Kevin's success in life has come from his deep relationship with God. Through these times of epic battles that are unthinkable or something you've seen in a movie, they have been real life to Kevin. Betrayed by friends, wounded by love ones, and yet he still holds fast to his integrity and his commitment to the lost and hurting. Has his badge tarnished? If so it just needs a little polish because he is still a hero in my life. I consider him a partner, a friend, and even a brother. A verse from the Bible comes to mind—Proverbs 17:17 a friend loves at all times, and a brother is born for adversity.

Jason Mueller was an incredible individual. He is the cousin of Jamie Peters whom I mentioned earlier in this book about his unsolved murder. Jason and I have known each other now since 1993. He is now married and has three incredible children. His wife is a general manager for Office Depot and he works for a Defense Contractor. Jason and I have been through a lot together. I remember his wedding, and his joining the U.S. Air Force. He began having seizures while in the Air Force which took a toll on him. No matter what, through it all, Jason remains faithful to his family, and to God. Jason has been an incredible friend.

Lalo Gunther was an impressionable fourteen-year-old and was being drawn into the local street gang in his neighborhood. I knew from day one that he had a good head on his shoulders; however, he lacked a father to provide structure and discipline. I arrested Lalo a number of times, and in the last case Lalo spent some time at the California Youth Authority. Lalo and I kept in  touch throughout the years, having our good times and bad. We have been through so much which forged and cemented our friendship like never before. He is now married to Dara, a wonderful young woman who is a college student, majoring in education. Lalo is a warehouse manager and attends college so he can become a school teacher as well. Lalo and I remember so many lessons from the past. He has grown so much. I cannot even tell you the stressful times of worrying about him when he was living the lifestyle of a gangster. I can remember shedding tears many nights while I would pray for him. Here is Lalo's recollection of how our paths crossed:

> *I remember hanging out in the quad with my "homeboy" Topo. This was at Chaparral High school in the early nineties. As we stood there a cop came up to us and started to talk with Topo as if they were friends. I immediately felt uncomfortable, because where I come from cops are not your friends. This cop asked Topo, "who's your friend?" This completely drove me away. And so I told Topo that I would catch up with him later. Little did I know*

that God would place a burden in the heart of this cop, for a young gang-
ster such as me.

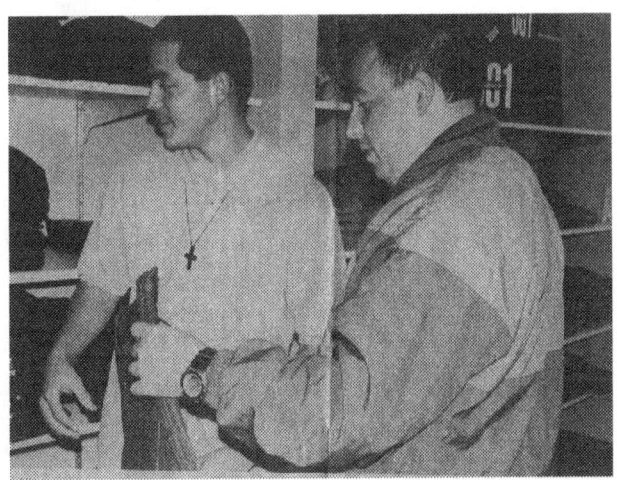

After that first encounter for some reason I began to see this cop on a frequent basis. I soon learned that he was the cop assigned to the gangs in our
city and that his name was Kevin. Kevin would often drive down our street
(Leslie Rd.) in an attempt to get to know this group of people and what we
were up to. He finally stopped one time and I hung around to see what he
was like. I thought he was different from what I expected as I began to read
his every move. Kevin came across as one who wanted to be a friend, which
caused me to lay down my guard.

I was not brought up a Christian so for me Bible study was a foreign concept. My homeboy Lil' Silent invited me to a Bible study one night. He told
me that Kevin was the one who would be taking him and a lot of others went
as well. So that night I waited outside of my apartments for a white Ford
Ranger with a camper shell to pick me up. They told me to hop in the back
with some others and so I did feeling very uncomfortable. "I am riding with
a cop," I said inside of my head. Never did I think this would be the case.

It was the ride home that I remember most vivid because I rode in the
front of the truck next to Kevin. He kept trying to get me to talk, but I
wasn't about to let down my guard completely. Kevin had a strict policy in
his truck that didn't allow for our type of music. However, somehow I got
him to ok my CD, which played the song "Eighteen with a Bullet." After he
had heard multiple expletives he finally ejected the CD and told me that
was why he didn't play other people's music in his car.

From this time forward things were changing, I began to go to these "Bible Study" groups almost on a weekly basis. Though I didn't fully understand what was being communicated at these studies. For me however, what drew me to attend was the fact that a lot of my friends were going and there were so many girls who also went. Kevin now was becoming more than just an acquaintance, he was becoming someone who I could trust. This led us to have many one on one times together, and my heart was open to his influence.

My upbringing as a child was tough, for I lacked many things that a child needed. I didn't grow up in a loving household where I could share my feelings or even be accepted for who I was. Instead I learned how to survive and make it without getting hurt by others. Without a dad around and my being bounced from house to house, I did not have stable teachers or mentors or even people who I thought cared for "me."

It wasn't until the latter part of my sixth grade year in school that my mom was able to get on welfare. This allowed my mom to put me and my four siblings all under the same roof once again. The apartments we moved to were located right in the "ghetto." There lived close to fifty gang members, most of who were close to the same age as me. At first I choose not to associate with any of them. I had my own group of friends. Eventually I began to establish a relationship with this group and later they became like my family.

My desires in life changed, no longer did I just do what was innocent and fun but I wanted to please this new group of "family" members. I wanted to be the most notorious kid on the block, and to be recognized as a leader. So I began to follow my peers and shun my real family, my siblings. This is right about the time Kevin came into my life. He was able to read all this from looking at me and wanted to help me.

Kevin tried many things to break the ties I had to my "gang family," but to no avail at first. I remember him saying to me one time, "List the most important things in your life." I thought that's easy. First it's my friends, and then it's my family, then maybe my girlfriend. Kevin said, "For me it's God, then from there everything follows." I thought, that's crazy, God first how can that be? As he explained it to me, God had to be first, so He could empower one to give to others.

I would spend many hours with Kevin and attend many outings with him. But I was still a gang member at heart and enjoyed it. I began to get into trouble, which resulted in Kevin having to get tougher with me. I was arrested a couple of times and so the city gave me a curfew. Kevin decided that he would photocopy a picture of me and hand it out to the police units on night patrol. He informed them that if they spotted me outside after 6pm they could arrest me. Kevin also tried to pull me out of the ghetto by having me live with a couple from Church. Even though I would be away from the gang life at night, I still had time to be who I wanted at school.

It was also during these times that Kevin would have to arrest me and take me to juvenile hall. An ordeal that Kevin said was very tough for him. I saw a new side to Kevin through this. Although he arrested me and sent me to that awful place, I still would hear from him. He would come into visit me and continue to pour out his heart. He even would convince me to make a change and I would agree. But the minute I would be released back to the ghetto, I would go right back to the gangs.

It wasn't until 1995 after being incarcerated on four different occasions, and had just been released from a nine month sentence that I would start to challenge my life style. All the ideas and influences from Kevin began to blossom from inside of me. I remember being at a party in El Cajon. While everyone danced, I just laid there on the couch. Everyone was saying to me, "Shaggy, what's going on, lets party." I had been known to be the center of attention and one who would always be on the dance floor. But this night something was happening to me. As I looked at all my "friends" I thought, "This is what life has to offer, just a splash of enjoyment, just a life lived like kids with no direction." I said, "This is not the way I want to live my life, I want more, I want reality."

As the dominoes began to fall in one direction it was like God was speaking to me without hesitation. The strong impact Kevin placed on my heart was moving me to question and understand life in a whole new way. God then allowed many tough and hard situations to transpire. I once again found myself incarcerated, this time it was for something major. Just days before, I had knelt down on my bed and said to God, "I cannot change out here, I need to be incarcerated, I need something major to happen in order for me to make a change." God answered that prayer in three days.

It was mid July of 1995, when everything completely changed for me. I was wrestling with what decision to make in my life. Whether I was going to continue the way I had for years or was there something on the other side. Because of Kevin's influence I knew beyond a shadow of a doubt that God existed. I knew also that I was not one of God's children, I served my own desires. So that July after much wrestling in my heart I stuck my head between a little window sill and said, "God if you are real—change my heart and life." That was all it took and my whole life was turned upside down.

I can sit back today and remember the many testimonies of individuals that have been touched by my life. God worked through me because of one man. The impact Kevin had in my life will never be forgotten or erased. Because of his faithfulness to stand for truth and be counted as a man of integrity, his legacy has been felt by countless others. I in turn seek to resemble those qualities in my life. I want to leave a mark on the hearts of people that will never be forgotten. I will never forget that mark that was left on my heart by one faithful man.

Harley Gunther has been an incredible blessing for my life. Harley and I can relate in so many ways that others cannot. We both share some of the same challenges in life. Watching Harley grow over the years has been such an incredible experience. Harley is the brother of Lalo who I spoke about earlier in this chapter. Harley has matured so much and has so much compassion for others. He has embarked on outreaches in Ireland and Mexico. Harley is a strong light. When he touches your life, you will never forget him. Here is his story:

I never would have thought that an El Cajon Police Officer would make such a huge impact in my childhood and teenage years. I met Kevin at age seven, when he was serving on the El Cajon Police Department. My brother, a former troublemaker, was always getting into trouble. So, Kevin, being a police officer, always responded to my neighborhood area. Kevin had responded to our neighborhood so much, that my family and I were able to become close with him.

Kevin, soon after finding out that five kids were in the family and fatherless, began to make an impact with my siblings and me by being that great father figure we never had. He took us hiking, out to lunch, and movies. Most importantly, he helped me by being that father figure that I needed when I needed someone to talk with about serious things. Growing up without a father was hard at times, but I knew that Kevin was someone I could depend on.

I was considered to be a rebellious child and during that time Kevin was trying to show me that being a bad rebellious child was a wrong act on my part. I use to shoplift, start fires in public places, curse at my mother, fight with others, have attitudes, and vandalize public property. These were just some of the activities I was involved in.

During this time, at age thirteen, I needed something more than just a father to help me get out of this era so in 1996 Kevin invited me to a small Church right down the street from where I lived. I was now surrounded by

Christian people with good morals and good attitudes. It's something I needed. I needed to be around good people. I soon became a regular at Calvary Chapel Lakeside and I started to see that God was real and that life was more than just being rebellious and cursing at people just because you wanted to. I now realized that God loved me and that there was a reason why I was living. Before having a relationship with God, I was depressed and confused. I am thankful to Kevin for leading me to a personal relationship with Jesus. I made a sincere commitment to God in June of 1998.

Since that time, God has shown me the reasons that he put Kevin in my life. He has still been there for me since I was seven. He has still been that father figure for me. This has shown me how great God is at putting people in your life for a reason. It boggles my mind to think of that. God would bring two people together like that for a specific purpose. Kevin did ask to be that father figure, he volunteered.

Finally, I just want to say that God gave us a purpose to live, and He has given Kevin a purpose in leading others, a leader to people who are in need. Kevin loves to be around people. I love you Kevin, and always will. I thank God for the experiences we have shared together and the things God has in store for us in the future.

David Rios became involved in our boxing program when he was fifteen. He had great talent and artistic ability. Over the years our friendship has grown. We stuck together through good times and bad. David is now a proud husband and father. I can remember during rough times, David would put his arm around me and tell me everything would be ok.  He always said, "I still love you bro!" Man, did that mean a lot and carry me through some of the darkest times of my life.

David Rios stood by me no matter what. I thank God for him even now as we grow closer each day that passes. We are family, and David knows what friendship is all about.

I met Kevin during the summer of 1993. I had just started the 10th grade. One day a friend told me that there was a boxing club not very far from school. He said it was a nice place. Since I was very much interested in boxing I decided to check the place out. I was real excited because one of my biggest dreams was to join some sort of boxing organization.

That afternoon right after school I decided to check the place out and see if it was really all I heard it would be. I also liked the fact that the gym was only three blocks away from my house. The gym was so popular for the fact that it had such a different, and positive, atmosphere.

The first day I went all my friends were there. As soon as I had entered the gym, I felt right at home. It was very clean and the people that were in charge of organizing the gym were very friendly. Kevin was then introduced to me for the first time. I didn't know that he was a peace officer for the city of El Cajon, let alone that he planned out, set up, and ran the gym on a daily basis.

It was obvious to everyone that I had been there for the first time but there was something about the staff, their entire attitude and demeanor was so different and outgoing, that it was almost like something out of a book or movie. Kevin was a very gracious and caring person; something that I didn't expect from him for the reason that he was an El Cajon Police Officer.

We had an awkward relationship at first, somewhat uncomfortable. He was very strict in the rules. It took a couple weeks and I started to see things in a different way and I realize that this guy was serious about improving the community by actually doing something great for it. Not just the community but for us, who at the time were lost souls and considered outcasts to the rest of society and were looking for guidance and a positive role model in our lives.

Bridge the Gap was a great program that will always hold a special place in my mind, just as the person who created it, will always have a special place in my heart. The next year Kevin was elected to the Grossmont Union High School District Board of Education. Being an elected official was not going to be an easy task. But in my mind I knew that he was going to give his best effort for he is not a man who would start something and live it half way through. That's not the friend I know. He is a man who is very determined in what he believes.

He thought that the students needed more than what we were already learning. During his time on the board, he was going to look into the most important things for students and not just administration. Therefore he thought that something needed to be done. At first it seems funny knowing that he was going to be running for the school board because I thought he was joking about it and was not being serious. I later realized that he meant business.

When he was elected I was very happy. That was another triumph for him and at the same time a great example for all of us. He was one of the greatest role models I have ever known in my entire life, and he still is. During his four years on the school board, he went through a lot of stressful times. There were sometimes when he wanted to give up and forget about the whole thing and not be part of it. He realized that during his most painful situations he was never left alone for there always was someone who he could count on, his very best friends. It is interesting that when I first met Kevin, I did not like his strict attitude. Later, we became best of friends, as we still are today.

Kevin has accomplished many things and still more things to come. He has true faith in God. Over the years I have been able to share the deepest things with Kevin. Never did he reject me or look down on me; he stood at my side and helped me through the low times in my life. He also trusted me with very deep things. Our sharing bonded our friendship like never before. Having said all this, I know that he doesn't hear this much, but all I want to say is that I love him so much and I'm thankful to God for having given me a friend like Kevin M. LaChapelle.

Prawitt Hess was seventeen, and his life's journey was dramatic. He was brought from Thailand to the U.S., and was separated from his mother for many years. They are now reunited, and she lives with Prawitt and his family. Prawitt is a firefighter, husband, and father. We have been through a lot. I can recall one time when Prawitt was being passed over for promotion and had evidence that it was based on discriminatory practice. After interviewing many of his fellow firefighters, I was stunned to learn that they too had heard many comments from supervisors that discriminated against Asian's, Latino's, and African American's. I represented him on behalf of SIA in a grievance hearing. I was ready for a rubber stamped process at the hearing and thought we would have to litigate this in court. I was pleasantly surprised that the hearing actually went in our favor. The panel sided with us and implemented new controls within their organization at our request to insure that the discriminatory practices did not happen again. Prawitt continues to work as a firefighter for the State of California and is doing well.

Moises Fraire joined our program when he was 15 years old. He was involved in Tagging (graffiti) and was put into an alternative education program. Moises and I have always had such a special friendship. Moises is now a machinist, drives big rigs, and enjoys taking care of his nieces. He plans to go back to school, something I have encouraged him to do. We have kept in touch over the years. Moises has and always will be such a pillar in my life. Even now when we talk, we recall how much we have been through and I continue to tell him how thankful I am for his friendship and loyalty.

David Gastelum has a wife and four kids. I can remember a time when I was speaking at Southwestern College. I brought him along. During my speaking, I could see David listening intently. After we left, he shed some tears and we had a heart to heart talk. I will never forget that talk we had. I always had incredible respect for David. He has such a genuine heart. Even now it is blessing when we get together. He is such a good father.

Raul and Leti Flores are an incredible family. I met Raul when he was involved in a fight. He was about 14 years old and just dabling into the gang scene. One day I met with his family to discuss my concerns over his behavior. I found his parents to be very responsive to my concerns. They decided to move Raul back to Tecate, Mexico. His family invited me to Tecate, Mexico, and this is what set my heart on fire for the Country of Mexico. Raul is now in his late twenties, married with two

children, and he and his wife own and operate a pharmacy in Tecate. They are best friends, and it shows in the family they are raising. It is a blessing to see the fruits of their labor. They recently completed building their new home. Raul is so full of business savy and wisdom from his father. They consider me part of their family, and I consider them a part of my family.

Sion Brannon was fifteen years old, and he was heavily entrenched in gang culture. He endured a lot, including being the victim of a shooting when he was eighteen. His mother and I encouraged him to leave San Diego and start over. Sion not only started over but also he earned his Bachelor of Science degree in Mathematics at Cal Poly. He then went on to obtain his teaching credential, and is now teaching Junior High in San Jose, California. Sion has persevered against great odds to succeed in life as well as in his career. It is such a pleasure to have dinner with him now and talk about his career as a school teacher and his impact on the young people he is leading.

Jose Orozco was just 17. He lost his mother to cancer when he was just eight years old and his father to the same disease when he was thirteen. Jose dropped out of school and was headed in the wrong direction when we met. He had bounced from one relative to another in search of a home. Mentoring Jose was an incredible experience. He needed someone who had faith in him, who genuinely cared about what happened to him, but more than anything, believed in him and his ability. Soon Jose obtained his G.E.D., then graduated from City College, then from San Diego State University and will now attend law school. Jose is one of our dedicated volunteers at S.I.A. Jose is committed to mentoring his cousins so that they will have the opportunity to experience a caring relationship with an adult concerned with their welfare. Jose stood by my side through it all, and has been the best friend I have ever had. He has held me accountable more than anyone ever has. He has been very instrumental in my returning to college to seek higher education. The bottom line is that Jose had impacted my life more than anyone ever had. He helped me work through so much scaring that I had suffered at the hands of the police department. I was able to share with him my weaknesses, and he listened and helped me get back up. Here is a note from Jose and what Mentorship has meant to him:

You only get a chance like this once in a lifetime. You buy tickets every week and then wait anxiously for the next day to see if you hit the jackpot. I didn't win the lottery that night but I also didn't buy a lottery ticket either. In fact I never bought one. That night, however, was my luckiest day. I was working at a Jack in the Box in North Park. I was fairly new on the job and was just getting the hang of things. While taking orders in the front register, a group of people walked in. "Big deal huh," groups of people always walk into a Jack in the Box. Oh no, these were not just any group of individuals, with them was a special person, one who only God knew would change me forever.

Kevin LaChapelle and his friends walked in to have dinner. They played a joke on me. Kevin told me that one of his friends was Arabic and told me his name, one that I could not pronounce. A few minutes after they left I received a call from "Jack". At the end of the conversation Jack was being impersonated by Kevin. He told me that if I ever wanted to hang out with them to give him a call and gave me his phone number.

During that time of my life, I was going through very dark days. I had recently dropped out of high school and was just beginning my life as an adult but quickly realized that working at a Jack in the Box was not something I wanted to do for the rest of my life.

A few weeks later, we went to a rappelling trip and soon afterwards we became regular acquaintances. We went to lunch every once in a while and discussed many things about life and the world. I realized that the world was bigger than what I thought it was. This is the problem with young people who are convinced that reality is their life in gangs, violence, and/or drugs. They do not know that the world is bigger than that.

On one occasion, Kevin gave me a gift for my birthday, a Bible. Even though I had grown up Catholic and went to Church every Sunday as a young child, I did not believe much in the religion itself. The timing of the Bible was perfect. As mentioned before, I was going through very dark days. I began to submerge myself in the bible and realized many things about our relation to God. I found many inconsistencies about Church and God Himself. For example, Churches depend on a few spiritual leaders who then guide the rest of the Church. The Bible, however, tells the individual to seek God Himself and not others to guide them to him. This might just show what condition our society is in when individuals seek the Church to get to God when in fact all they need to do is seek God. I am not denying the importance of accountability or of a support system, but am discrediting the dependence some people place on someone else's faith.

Kevin and I debated on many things about the Bible and there were times where I would accept his argument and there were others where he seemed to agree with me. It seemed as though as my relationship with Kevin was growing so was my relationship with God. I am not implying in any way that Kevin is the way to God but that God sent me a good friend such as Kevin.

Up to this day I always consider myself an extremely fortunate person to have met Kevin. I am convinced that God crossed our paths so that we can together live this life which at times seems so useless. Everywhere one turns there is corruption. Many believe that we have the best government system in the world. I would argue that any government system which is governed by humans is corrupt. There is no surprise then, that Kevin has seen and exposed corrupt systems in our government.

We would like to believe that things will get better in our nation. This, however, will not happen until, like Kevin, others rise up to expose and change the current corrupt systems. The status quo is strong because just like the young people who are convinced that their world is reality in which they cannot get out of, we at times are also convinced that ours is reality and that there is no other. It is up to you and me to decide what our future reality will be.

Luis Castillo exemplifies his role as a husband and father. He is so loyal to his family that many of his peers look to him as an example as to how they need to lead their own families. Luis, his wife and child are a blessing to us all. His genuine and consistent love for God and family stands out in a world where families are so  often split apart. Luis has such a genuine heart, and is such a loyal friend. I thank God for his friendship. I really enjoy the times Luis, Lucia, and Luisito come over to spend time singing and just hanging out. All of the mountain bike rides, hiking trips, and Thanksgiving and Christmas dinners, are just incredible.

Agustin Pena is quite the young man. He is a full time college student committed to either becoming a school teacher or an attorney. From the time we met, I could tell he was sincere in his passion to be there for others and rise up alongside the weak.

Growing up, we all had someone whom we admired and idolized. For some it was their father or father-like figure. For most it was some sort of fictional character in which we needed to find emotional comfort and refuge in. Heroes come in many different shapes and many different sizes. We look up to them regardless of their physical characteristics. What we see as a hero is someone who stands up for justice and the good of humanity at any cost. In the world of fiction there is an endless amount of characters that have these attributes. Unfortunately we cannot say the same for us and the world that we live in today. I feel that by the day there are less and less people who fight for what is right, and when someone does, the second that it starts to get a bit messy they flee with their tails in between their legs like a scolded dog. The irony is that the group that states that they are here to serve and protect by upholding the law with the utmost of integrity, pee all over us as a canine would do to mark its territory. They are known to talk victims out of pursuing criminal charges by methods of intimidation, and give criminals the "benefit of the doubt" instead of the victims. I myself was pushed to one side and completely discredited after I had gone to the police after my 12 year old brother had been robbed at knife point. I managed to take the officer to the scene of the crime, which was also the suspect's domain, and all he said was that "There's not much I can do".

Those of us with a socially conscious mind, constantly, ask ourselves with the moral decay of today's society, who is going to emerge from the crowd to stand firm for a just cause? I never really knew the answer to that, or that such a character existed, until I met Kevin. Kevin M. LaChapelle is notorious for aiding those who are in need. No matter the degree of their troubles, Kevin has always been the first to volunteer to lend a helping hand, especially for his friends. Such a person is extremely rare in this world; most people are about what they can get out of the situation for themselves. Kevin has always been a selfless and very contributing person and never asking for anything in return. In the eyes of many Kevin is a hero, including my own, for the constant pursuit of good overcoming evil. He is compelled to help the weak from becoming victimized. His generosity, kindness, and sincerity is a very rare combination of attributes in one person, all he needs now is a cape. Such a person with a heart the size of his, only exists in stories and that is why I am glad I can call him my friend.

Although not that publicly known, at least not as it should be, police corruption is a very serious and controversial topic. Corruption is the very cancer that eats away at a city neighborhood by neighborhood. Unfortunate as the events that Kevin has experienced have been, he may now expose the police for what they truly are. Deceptive, socially-crippling, parasites!

James Velasquez is a very unique individual. When I first met James, he was ready to take off for the military. I have found that many young people join the military for all of the wrong reasons. I believe people should have accurate information before making life decisions such as a career in the military. James has so much compassion for his friends and even strangers. He is a person that many people confide in as they know they can trust him. That very trust is what I appreciate so much in James. Here is his story of how we met:

I didn't care what my parents thought about me. I wanted to be a U.S. Marine. I liked the uniform and I loved the sword the marines showed in the commercials. I loved the fact that every marine had at least two to three girlfriends and if they got the chance to travel, they always made a new girlfriend in the places they traveled in. If I joined the Marine Corps it would mean no more school for me. But at the same time I wanted to be a peace officer. I wanted to help out the community. I wanted to stop abusive parents who would hit their children or those who physically abused their wives.

I remember that my friend Agustin Pena called me and asked me if I could meet him at the Denny's located in City Heights. He told me he wanted to introduce me to a friend of his named Kevin. Since I was off that day I told him that I would love to meet Kevin. As I was walking into the Denny's restaurant I spotted Agustin and my friend from high school. It was Agustin Pena and Oscar Arce, both sitting in the same seat and having a conversation with two gentlemen. As I approached the table I remember sitting with Oscar and Agustin, facing the other two gentlemen who introduced themselves as Kevin LaChapelle and Jose Orozco.

After having a normal conversation between Kevin and myself, Kevin asked me what were my goals for life. I told him I wanted to be a Marine. He immediately asked me why I wanted to be a Marine. I was quiet for a couple of minutes. Obviously I wanted to make a good impression of myself so I did not tell Kevin why I really wanted to be a Marine. I knew the answer right off the top of my head, to have million and billions of girlfriends because that's what Marines do. But his question also made me wonder if becoming a Marine was really the career for me? I never answered his question but I did mention that college was free if I joined the military.

That's when Jose started to laugh. Jose then asked me if that's why I wanted to join the military, because they paid for my college. I told him yes, obviously I was lying. Jose said that if I really wanted to go to college, it would be best for me to go to City College. Jose and Kevin told me that San Diego City College actually paid for your classes if you wanted to continue with school. Kevin also asked me what my alternative goal would be apart from becoming a Marine. I told him that I was also thinking of being a peace officer. I wanted to help out kids, the community, and stop abusive parents. After I informed him of my reasons he later told me that he himself was a former police officer. I wanted to ask Kevin a lot of questions! Like, what do I need to be a police officer? What are the requirements to become a police officer? Do I really have to go to an academy? A lot of questions started to come into mind. I was excited! That's when I started to realize that things didn't happen because they just happen.

I knew that God had done something to have Kevin in my life. If it wasn't for him I am certain that right now I would have been in Iraq fighting the war on terrorism with most of my friends from high school. It is sad to say that as of today I have not heard from any of my friends. I do have a friend that just came back from Iraq and he always tells me how happy he is that I did not join the military. He said that the recruiters lie about everything and that all they care about is the money they receive for recruiting people. His brother was going to follow his steps but as he told him what the real deal was, at the end his brother did not join the military.

My mom is constantly reminding me to never take my friends for granted. She is always telling me how grateful she is that I did not join the military, that she thanks God for letting me have awesome friends that care and love me as much as she does. My dad, who I hardly spoke to, one time told me that he thanks God for having Agustin Pena and Oscar Arce introduce me to Kevin LaChapelle and Jose Orozco. He even admitted that he did not want me to join the military. I never realized how much I had until I had this conversation with both of my parents.

As of today I am pleased to say that I did not join the Marine Corps. I am actually going to college! I mean me? The one that said I would never go to school even if they paid me too! Well, now the government is paying for my classes in order for me to keep going to college. I thank God for that very moment that I met Kevin at that Denny's restaurant in City Heights, and for showing Agustin Pena, Oscar Arce, and myself the right path to follow. Ever since then Kevin and everyone else have been caring for each other just like a family would.

Steve Gonzalez has been an incredible friend over the years. Steve has a heart for young people like I have never seen before. Steve is probably the most genuine individual I have ever known. Steve's sole purpose is to reach out to young people who do not see hope for their lives. He showed them the love God has for them, and he walks at their side encouraging them to seek God and all he has planned for their lives. Here are some words from Steve:

If you want to change the world, think small. It sounds so backwards to how our current society functions. When I think of Kevin LaChapelle I think of a man who started small and ended up touching so many lives.

When I think of some of the years that are covered in this book I am bombarded with certain memories. Memories that bring joy for my friend Kevin as well as memories that I know bring pain.

As a person who is committed to reaching kids on the fringe of society, I have a great deal of respect for Kevin and law enforcement personnel like him. I acknowledge that many times these young people are making decisions that are detrimental to themselves and society. As a young man I made many mistakes and made a mess of my teenage years. I remember being at the wrong end of the law many times. I can't think of one policeman during those years who expressed any type of compassion or who sought to understand me as a person. I probably didn't deserve to be treated with compassion for any reason other than the fact that I was a human being. When I met Kevin, I encountered a man who walked a fine line. A man of integrity who wore a badge; and at the same time still cared about people. He cared about those on the fringe of society. He cared for those who had lost their vision and purpose in life. But not only did he say he cared, he acted on what he said. He treated fairly those who needed to be arrested and had compassion for those who had been affected by those crimes.

I think of the years on the school board and the pain it caused him. Although I am not privileged to know everything that happened in the board room, I do know this: that Kevin acted in the best interest of the young people he served. He wanted young people to be served fairly and receive the education that they deserved. How that played out in public is open for debate but not his desire to help.

Kevin is one of my true heroes. I witnessed a young man act on what he believed. He wanted to make a difference in society and he took on the responsibilities of wearing a badge. He was a good cop. He thought young people desired a quality education and tried to help in that arena as well. I think the world would be a better place if more of us acted on what we truly believed. We may not always be right, but at least we're in the game. Kevin, thanks for being my friend.

Steve Gonzales
President/Founder Dream Weavers
www.dreamweaverssandiego.org

The following excerpts are letters of support I received from Tom Godley, Bill Walk, and Mike Eddy. When I read these letters, tears swept my eyes. These men are incredible and I have so much admiration for all of them and what they stand for. To receive their words was phenomenal for me.

When I first sent an email out inviting my close friends to be a part of this chapter, I received the following response from one of the true heroes at the school district, Bill Walk. Bill was the Assistant Superintendent of Human Resources. Bill is an incredible man with principle. The teachers union did everything in their power to destroy this man and others for his commitment to bettering public education. Anytime a person stands against the status quo, you can bet the attacks will begin. Many of these unsung heroes sacrificed everything, yet never are rewarded here in this world. I am certain that God is keeping good records. Here is the text from the email sent by Bill Walk:

It is amazing that a single person's name "LaChapelle" will bring so much emotion forward that it is positively overwhelming to me. What can I say Kevin?

My professional life is completely destroyed. Yet, with all that I have gone through; and, indirectly subjected my family, I would not have changed a single thing except the opportunity to have more time.

After Grossmont I was unable to find employment anywhere. Each and every time I applied for a job [usually 1 out of every 2 applications submitted] I would receive an interview. Invariably I would be a finalist. In some cases I was the only finalist [Chino, Truckee, Ontario Montclair, and others]. Then, a call would be placed either by the search chairman and or the president of the union to Grossmont. NO JOB. In one case, I was the finalist for two different jobs in two different departments in the same district and did not get the job. I had one Superintendent chase me out to my car and tell me I was exactly the person he was looking for and could I spend the night so that he could talk to his Board. Then he called me in my hotel room and told me he wanted to hire me but I would have been too controversial for the Board.

I then went through a bout of physical ailments including five surgeries. I now take weekly injections for arthritis which I believe can all be attributed to the hell I went through in simply trying to straighten out public education. Some believe viruses and or bacteria and or cancer to be the most destructive forces known to mankind. I would suggest that losing your home, not being able to be employable and see the look in your wife's eyes as you fail; and, then trying to make ends meet as two sons matriculate through college to be more destructive than any possible ailment created by virus, bacteria or cancer.

Regardless, I still look up in the sky and say: "I'm still here, I still am waiting, just give me a sign.

My wife and sons are really doing well. I am over the emotional part of my dilemma [except I did cry as I saw your name—it has been a long time since that happened]. I simply live, similarly to an alcoholic, "one day at a time." If I didn't have this f***ing pride I would have blown my brains out along time ago.

God be with you always Kevin. My plight, in comparison to what you sacrificed, is child's play. You are my hero.

I love you. Always have total respect for you. You showed me that I did not live in a vacuum in public education. For that I will always be indebted. There were times, very lonely times, when I thought I was the only person on the face of the earth who thought our public school system was destructive to children.

BW

The following letters were sent on my behalf to the law school which I had applied for admission. I have included these letters to show the tone for the seriousness of what occurred while I served as President of the Grossmont Union High School District Governing Board of Education. In addition, these fine men who have submitted these letters were incredible examples to me.

Letter of Support from Bill Walk

I first met Mr. LaChapelle when I became the Assistant Superintendent of Personnel for the Grossmont Union High School District. Mr. LaChapelle was a member of the Governing Board of Trustees for the school district. Mr. LaChapelle was directly responsible for restructuring the school district's central office administration, recruiting the new superintendent, bringing outside the district school agencies into the district, and seeking outside law enforcement assistance in reviewing the district's legal practices.

Mr. LaChapelle single handedly uncovered not only poorly managed and administered administrative practices; he was able to assist outside legal sources in bringing legal action against the school district. Obviously, during the turmoil, as described, the newly hired central administration worked closely with the Governing Board. It was through this long and arduous process that enabled me to best understand Mr. LaChapelle's qualifications as a leader; and, most importantly, as a citizen.

Whenever there is corruption uncovered in any institution, especially a school district, an entirely new set of dynamics are established. It was through Mr. LaChapelle's leadership as the Governing Board's President, that the school district was literally able to reinvent itself and survive the potential takeover by the County Office of Education. In other words, Mr. LaChapelle's uncommon valor, which was at great risk to his professional standing and personal well-being, literally allowed the school district to remain under local control.

There was no doubt that Mr. LaChapelle possessed the necessary legal background, as a police officer, to remain true to his core values when he was elected to the Governing Board. However, it was not until he was confronted by the Governing Board majority and the former superintendent, who was well aware that Mr. LaChapelle suspected corruption within the district, that I believe Mr. LaChapelle discovered his inner-most strength. This confrontation resulted in personal threats, he was restricted in access to schools and district data, and was not included in Governing Board activities. Obviously, this created a tension in the district; but, did not deter Mr. LaChapelle from seeking the truth. After a two year torturous process, Mr. LaChapelle prevailed. A new Governing Board majority was elected and a new superintendent was brought into the district to provide much needed leadership. Mr. LaChapelle was famous for saying: "It makes no matter the personal set backs I have endured; this district will never revert to what it was; and, will never ever be the same."

Mr. LaChapelle is a principle centered individual, who is highly intelligent, and very tenacious when he suspects that citizens, locally or nationally, are being betrayed by those who they have bestowed trust and confidence. Mr. LaChapelle has an easy going style or manner; yet, when he feels invigorated by a challenge or, as stated, if he views an injustice, he will work tirelessly to serve the needs of others.

As a side note, Mr. LaChapelle constantly works with those who are less fortunate. He has worked to provide assistance to young people in need of guidance in the San Diego area; and, he has worked towards bringing services to Mexicans in Mexico. This side note provides another window into Mr. LaChapelle's soul. No matter how well off or how in need of help Mr. LaChapelle may be, he always has time for others no matter their predicament or their background. To say that Mr. LaChapelle practices what he preaches would definitely be an understatement.

Mr. LaChapelle's application to the Thomas Jefferson School of Law is a natural evolution of his professional development. As a former police officer, a leader of other police officers, his intimate relationships with attorneys representing the Grossmont Union High School District, and the obvious success he achieved in "righting" a woeful school district it would be perfectly natural for him to secure additional accreditation to "right the wrongs" that he is so passionate about.

Mr. LaChapelle receives my highest recommendation in support of his desire to attend your law school. Please do not hesitate to contact me should you want additional information regarding Mr. LaChapelle's capabilities. A warning, however, you will hear more of the same. Mr. LaChapelle remains one of my all-time civic heroes. We need more people, such as Mr. LaChapelle, who unselfishly provides time and heroically meets the challenges within our society today.

Most sincerely,

William E. Walk, III

Letter of Support from Tom Godley

It is a privilege to write this letter for Kevin LaChapelle. I have had the distinct pleasure of being associated with Kevin, both professionally and personally, since 1997. This association began when I was hired as Superintendent of Schools for the Grossmont Union High School District in February of 1997 and has continued until the present. Kevin was a School Board Member when I was hired, and subsequently was voted by his colleagues to serve as Board President in November of 1997. Before coming to Grossmont, I also served as Superintendent in San Marino Unified School District. More recently, I served as a full-time associate professor and director of the doctoral program in educational leadership at Azusa Pacific University. Just this year, I "un-retired" and came back to K-12 public education, as Assistant Superintendent of Business Services in the Orange Unified School District.

During my 34 years in education, I have had the opportunity to observe and work with numerous board members. Kevin LaChapelle stands out as an exemplary role model among his peers. During his tenure Kevin guided the Board with integrity, wisdom, compassion and courage. His background includes being an officer with the El Cajon Police Department, and serving as an investigative consultant in the private sector. While serving as a police officer, Kevin specialized in working with at-risk youth in the community and was once recognized as policeman of the year for those efforts.

Prior to me being selected as superintendent, Kevin was instrumental as a board member in recommending a special investigative audit of the district's business practices and procedures for internal controls. As soon as I took office, he convinced me of that same recommendation, and an in-depth special audit was immediately conducted. The results showed some 43 findings and recommendations ranging from minor irregularities to major violations of circumventing the public bidding requirements, and lack of full disclosure to the board for various contracts and business arrangements. The recommendations of both special investigative audits have been implemented; the business practices have been completely reformed; and, tighter internal controls are now in place.

In conclusion, Kevin has demonstrated an exceptional aptitude for the study of law, the strength of character, and the interpersonal skills to be an excellent student and attorney. It is with pleasure and without equivocation that I recommend Kevin LaChapelle as student in your law school.

Sincerely,

Thomas A. Godley, Ed.D.
Superintendent, Orange Unified School District

Letter of Support from Mike Eddy

The focus of this letter is to provide a letter of introduction on behalf of Mr. Kevin LaChapelle.

Mr. LaChapelle's previous experience as a police officer for the City of El Cajon and his community service as President of the Grossmont Union High School District Board of Trustees places him at the top of the ladder. In addition, he established a non profit Corporation (Special Investigations Agency) designed specifically to assist and support the elderly and immigrants who were targeted for financial fraud. His dedication and numerous contributions to our community have made a significant and successful impact.

Mr. LaChapelle's character is beyond reproach. Integrity, loyalty and commitment are the hallmarks of Mr. LaChapelle's persona. In addition to the above, Mr. LaChapelle has the ability to extract the relevant from the irrelevant which is a required skill in the practice and study of the law. On numerous occasions the undersigned has observed these skills in which Mr. LaChapelle stands above the crowd.

Mr. LaChapelle has the requisite skills and qualifications to study law. His perseverance in all tasks he has undertaken exhibit his commitment and dedication to achieving his goals.

Mr. LaChapelle is strongly endorsed for your consideration as a student to study law at Thomas Jefferson School of Law.

Sincerely,

Michael F. Eddy
Juris Doctor
Colonel, USMC (Ret'd)

All of these people were brought into my life by God for very specific reasons. Each time I felt abandoned by God, He would send the most remarkable people into my life. Words cannot begin to describe the incredible friendships God has established in my life. Often times, during the first few moments of meeting someone, I would have a clear vision of how this person could be used by God for good and to have an impact in this world.

Interestingly, while I was seated as the elected president of a school board, some of the best friends that stood by my side through it all were looked down upon by many as Mexican immigrants. These Mexican friends were a lifeline from God! The loyalty they had shown me never ceases to amaze me. I thank God daily for these true heroes in my life.

With all that I have been through, I am reminded daily of who I am, what I stand for, and why God has allowed me to experience all that He has. Every time I begin to take my eyes off of God, I am quickly reminded that without God, I am nothing.

CHAPTER ELEVEN

And Here We Stand...

As this book has revealed, I have many friends and many enemies. I have learned a great deal from both. I have tried to fight for what is right and stand up when I see injustice. At times it has been difficult for me when people became critical of my actions having never heard the actual account of what had transpired. I do not mind criticism; in fact I have a quote in my office that goes like this, "If both of us agree on everything, one of us needs to go!" It is however difficult when criticism is coming from a position of misinformation.

I now see life much different than when I was sworn in as a police officer in 1989. I now realize how fragile people are, how vulnerable this world is, and see the failures in institutions. Institutions are made up of people, and people are imperfect. I have learned that people who proclaim their righteousness are also very capable of evil. I have learned how people entrusted to protect others, often betray that trust because of their selfishness and arrogance. I have seen this failure within the institution of government and religion most. It surprises me how many people place their trust in government and religious institutions instead of putting their trust in the only one not capable of failing us, God!

My relationship with God has vastly changed. The closer I am drawn toward God, the more I recognize my shortcomings. I have learned that institutions will fail us; however we can rely on God and the people He places within our lives. Many people set themselves up for failure by putting their faith in pastors and mega churches instead of genuinely developing a relationship with God on their own. They are more concerned with what church a person attends than with actually having an intimate and relevant relationship with God. God wants to show Himself to us daily in all He does for us, and all of the doors He opens for us to impact others. I see God at work in everything, everyday. Some see things as coincidence, when many know it is God!

As for the El Cajon Police Department, they have a new police chief as of 2005, Clifford Diamond. The last time a chief was brought in from the outside to clean things up, it was Jack G. Smith. From 1995 until 2005 the department had been led by the circle that held its tight reign on the department for years creating and fostering an environment that almost encouraged corrupt behavior. In addition, the City of El Cajon has a fairly new city manager, Kathi Henry. Hopefully the new city manager along with the city council will be steadfast in holding the new police chief accountable in ridding the police department of its corrupt culture. Of course change does not occur overnight. The new chief will need support from the community to change the culture within the police department.

Just prior to this book being released in February 2006, yet another El Cajon Police Officer was just charged with eight felony counts of sexual misconduct.

The culture of corruption is held together by the clique at the top of the police department that has continued to hold its tight grip of power and control for several decades. Chief Diamond will need strong community support and prayer to rid the El Cajon Police Department of its culture of corruption.

In Summary...

This is my first attempt at writing a book. Never did I realize what I was in for. This would be no easy task, especially for an author that is both ADHD and has somewhat of a rebellious nature. I have tried to document many events that have transpired during my life so that others could see how God had never left my side, even though at times I thought He had abandoned me.

I hope that while reading this book you were able to see how God has used even the most unlikely people to reach others. Many times I was right on target, yet many times I was way off. No matter what, God continued to show me the way and in the midst of my trials reached many people through my willingness to be transparent and available.

This book is probably not a traditional book. The editors would ask me, "Who is your target audience? Your book needs to be narrowed to reach a specific audience." I would be told, "Don't use the word 'God' in your title; it will narrow your audience even more." I shared this with my oldest sister Leslie. She said it well, "I am tired of people pushing God out of everything." I was advised by many to change the title to, "Don't Let My Badge Tarnish." I almost consented, until Leslie voiced her opposition. What she said really caused me to stand firm in my original title. I just could not remove the very God that stood by me through everything, and loved me when many would shun me.

For those who know me, they know that the more I am pressured in one area, the more I will do just the opposite. I guess my nonconformist attitude would not allow me to conform to what all of the professionals would tell me. The bottom line is that I just wanted this book to be from my heart. God has held me in the grips of His hands every step of my life, all the while showing me how much I needed to rely on Him and lean on His understanding and strength instead of my own. As I continue to fail myself and be failed by others, God stands firm!

Appendix A

January 23, 1994

Mr. Alan Crogan, Chief Probation Officer
San Diego County Probation Department
2901 Meadow Lark Drive
San Diego, California 92123

Dear Mr. Crogan,

I am writing this complaint about one of your probation officers, "M". You and I have spoken about this matter previously and I am now putting it in writing. I request that the Probation Department conduct an investigation and take appropriate disciplinary action.

There are several questionable actions taken by PO "M" that indicate that she took an extraordinary interest in my son Jesus case. I have learned that prior to my son's case being assigned to her, and before I knew Mr. Kevin LaChapelle, she stated that she wanted to get my son's case. Shortly after New Year 1994, she stated to him that she wanted my son's case to "get him" or "fix him" because she felt that I was using my position to get favorable recommendations from assigned probation officers on behalf of my son.

Prior to "M's" being assigned my son's case, he was supervised by PO "J". He had received a Camp commit upon a report submitted by PO Joana "W". No preferential treatment of my son's case has ever been given by these or any other probation officer's assigned.

Upon reassignment of the case to "M", she took it upon herself to violate the Court's orders and remove Jesus name from the YLC-possible list. See page "g" of report dated 7-14-94. The orders were quite clear and "M" either misunderstood the orders or just did not care to follow the court's order. Further, she did not bother to check the Court's intention either with the Court or with PO "J". This order included the plan to have my son complete the Camp and YCC programs and live with his brother and I in Santa Ysabel. I had nothing to do with seeking placement on the YDC list. Please speak to PO "J" about these facts.

My son was subsequently administratively removed from Camp and placed in Juvenile Hall. Ms. "M'"s recommendation was a commitment to the California Youth

Authority. There are many events that transpired during the Court process that need scrutiny. Specifically, "M" blatantly lied to the Court, under oath, and with the expressed intention of getting the Court to follow her CYA recommendation. Here we are talking about a calculated, precipitated felonious act. She knew what the truth was. Specifically, she and Mr. LaChapelle had discussed my son for a possible placement in his upcoming program. He told her that he would take my son into his program as he "was not a bad kid". Please review Court transcript pages 189-193. She unabashedly lied to the Court by saying facts she knew to be untrue. She lied about dates that she spoke with Mr. LaChapelle, about knowing that one of his program homes could be on-line by Oct/November 1994, and saying that Mr. LaChapelle had stated to her that he would not accept my son into his program because he would not be appropriate "because of his gang history."

I believe that "M" lied to the Court in an attempt to discredit my testimony during Court proceedings. In addition to the transcript, please talk to any of the court personnel that were present, including Senior PO Wayne "F".

"M's" motives and questionable activities could also include witness tampering as she, in conjunction with DA "H", attempted on two occasions to dissuade Mr. LaChapelle to speak the truth and to testify more along the lines of what "M" testified. The first incident took place following the hearing of July 29, 1994. She and DA "H" both spoke on the phone to Mr. LaChapelle. This was reported to my son's attorney, Frank "N", about the evening conversations with both "M" and DA "H".

The second incident took place on August 9, 1994, the day before Mr. LaChapelle was scheduled to testify and straighten out who was lying in Court, me or "M". They again tried to get him to change his testimony and threatened him if he didn't cooperate. The threats were related to his securing his group home permits. On August 10, 1994, DA "H" lied to the Court when he told the Court that he had received a telephone call from Mr. LaChapelle that he would be about five minutes late when he in fact told Mr. LaChapelle to wait in the DA'S office until he was called. Mr. LaChapelle came into the Courtroom to testify about 30 minutes after the start of the hearing.

Mr. LaChapelle is prepared to submit information and names of persons who were around him and "M" when she reference my son. He can also describe unfair, unprofessional treatment by "M" which includes slander of his name to other law enforcement officers.

Mr. Crogan, I am quite concerned about the creditability of the department when we have such questionable activity, verbal coercion, and slanting of the truth just to win a recommendation. I am concerned about the honesty and integrity of "M". I am seeking an ethical investigation.

Thank you in advance for investigating this matter and for keeping me informed of the progress. I will submit transcripts and reports. If I can be of further assistance, I will be glad to provide any information you may need.

Sincerely,

P.O. "G"

Appendix B

Sgt. Billy Cox
9/14/1994
Faxed from Dan Lamborn

REPORT AND INVESTIGATION
OFFICER K. LACHAPELLE—EL CAJON POLICE DEPARTMENT

The investigation and interviews conducted by Officer LaChapelle were incompetent and conducted in such a manner that were completely devoid of any objective fact finding. The facts that are relevant to this are that Officer LaChapelle tainted every aspect of this investigation so that the truth may never be known due to his contaminating every person he contacted with his personal assumptions.

Qualifications:
What training has Officer LaChapelle received in conducting internal affairs investigations? How many internal affairs investigations has he conducted?

What training has officer LaChapelle received in conducting investigations and interviews with sexual assault victims? How many investigations of sexual assaults has he conducted?

It appears that Officer LaChapelle is an officer of very limited police experience (five years or less) and that he has never served in the capacity of a detective. This lack of experience and training resulted in several critical mistakes.

El Cajon Police Dept. Policy and Procedure Manual:
It appears that officer LaChapelle violated several provisions of the P&P's while conducting this investigation. It appears that this officer was not authorized by any provision to conduct a personal investigation without the permission of the Chief of Police. In each of the following areas it will be detailed that not only was this investigation outside the standards set by ECPD, it violated most of the commonly practiced

techniques of investigation and interviewing used by police agencies in this county and the state.

The failure to follow department policy and commonly practiced police techniques resulted in a cascade effect that led to a predetermined outcome.

As a result of using improper techniques the truth and facts of this case may never be determined. The parties to this incident have been devoid of any spontaneous statements which resulted in the premature focusing of the investigation on the accused officer.

SUMMARY

EXPERIENCE:
Neither Officer LaChapelle or Moore have any experience in conducting internal affairs investigations.

Neither officer has any experience in conducting sexual assault investigations.

Both officers are patrol officers with very limited police experience.

POLICIES:
Both officers violated department policy on not one but several different times during the course of this incident. This crusade resulted in botched interviews and tainted facts. Had trained professional investigators operating with the permission and supervision of the police department conducted the investigation, the outcome might have been different.

INTERVIEWS:
The interview techniques used by Officers LaChapelle and Moore were incompetent at best. They compromised every interview by supplying the witness with information prior to obtaining a statement. This removed any possibility of a spontaneous statement from the witnesses which might have resulted in a different conclusion. The tape recording is only a partial record of the conversation with the alleged victim but there are no notes or reports to indicate what conversation took place that was not recorded. The victim is crying and sobbing when the tape starts, what was said to make her so emotional?

The officers failure to follow policy, failure to conduct a competent investigation (because they are not trained to conduct complex investigations) failure to document all conversations with the witnesses, tampering with the witnesses through improper and incompetent interview techniques, has tainted this case to the point where it might be impossible to get true and unbiased responses from the parties involved.

POLICE REPORT
OFFICER K. LACHAPELLE, ECPD

PARAGRAPH 1:
This conversation with Steveson took place on Saturday, a day off. for Officer LaChapelle, where did it take place?

What is the relationship between Steveson and LaChapelle? Are they friends? Do "they attend the same church? This is important later when credibility is assigned to statements by Steveson.

LaChapelle wrote that during a conversation Steveson mentioned that Kennedy was having sex with young girls? Who initiated the conversation about sex? This is critical to show that Officer LaChapelle might have been harboring some ill feelings towards Kennedy. If LaChapelle initiated the conversation then it also shows that he was incapable of conducting an unbiased investigation.

LaChapelle wrote that Steveson said that Kennedy said that he was having sex with a sixteen year old girl. When was Steveson told this? Did he in fact hear it directly from Kennedy or did he hear a rumor? Officer LaChapelle failed to ask any basic questions about the statements that he was reporting on from Steveson.

PARAGRAPH 3:
LaChapelle reported that he had heard rumors that Kennedy was sexually active with young girls. Is it the common practice of members of ECPD to engage in rumor baiting? Section 1.5, Page 1, item 1., "Members of this dept be courteous, civil, and respectful toward each other, and toward all persons on all occasions." It appears that based on the rumor conversation that took place in paragraph one and what was said in paragraph 3, Officer LaChapelle routinely violates this provision. Who did he hear these rumors from? When did he hear them? Was he on or off duty when he heard them?

It is critical that the last part of the first sentence in paragraph three is, "but did not put much reliability in it." Did he not put much reliability in it because of the untarnished reputation enjoyed by Officer Kennedy? Was it because the people who told him regularly gossip about fellow employees?

LaChapelle writes that after being told the information by Steveson he felt that it was a serious allegation that needed further investigation. Why did he dismiss the rumors before but now suddenly felt that it was a serious matter? This is very inconsistent with the prior statement.

Why did Officer LaChapelle assign such credibility to the statements of Steveson? Steveson had been dismissed from ECPD for improperly identifying himself as a ECPD employee during an argument in a public place.

PARAGRAPH 4:
The information was received on 04-23-94, why didn't Officer LaChapelle notify a superior officer of this "serious allegation". Two days later on 04-25-94, Officer LaChapelle still had not contacted a superior officer about this situation. This is a violation of Section 1.5, Page 4, item 20, subsection (d.):

> *Any duly commissioned officer of this dept while off duty, within or outside of the city limits of El Cajon, who is involved in any police activity, whether initiated by himself or others, shall immediately notify the Duty Watch Commander and prepare a detailed report of said incident with an El Cajon Police Dept case number. This report shall be submitted to the duty Watch Commander for review immediately.*
> *(d.): Activity of any nature which results in the officer identifying himself, or being identified by others as a peace officer.*

Section 2.3, Page 2, "The initial investigation of an incident leading to potential disciplinary action is to be conducted as assigned by the Chief of Police."

Before the investigation had even started, LaChapelle had violated three department directives. He routinely engaged in gossiping about fellow employees, he failed to notify immediately the watch commander or his superior officers of a serious incident, he initiated an internal affairs inquiry without the permission of the Chief of Police.

PARAGRAPH 4:

This is where the serious lapses of professional police investigative techniques started. When LaChapelle contacted the mother of the alleged victim he committed a serious interview error. He asked her if she had ever heard that Kennedy was involved with her daughter. There was no lead in. no preliminary questioning. A qualified investigator would have asked:

Are you aware that there are rumors that your daughter is sexually active?

Have you heard from your daughter or others whom she might be having sexual relations with?

Have you heard from your daughter or other persons that she might be having sexual relations with a member of the police dept?

Have you heard from your daughter or other persons who that police department employee might be?

Has your daughter ever mentioned having a relationship with Officer Kennedy?

By supplying the mother with the name of Officer Kennedy from the onset, he destroyed any chance of a spontaneous statement from the mother. What if she had another employee in mind but was reluctant to state so after being interviewed by LaChapelle. When conducting an investigation it is essential that the officer not direct the witness in a particular direction. A true and honest reaction to questioning can only be obtained when the witness is permitted to recall and express themselves in a manner that is free of influence by the interviewer.

PARAGRAPH 5:

Officer LaChapelle was contacted by Officer Moore who is the brother-in-law of the alleged victim. He had received a call from his mother-in-law about the incident. Now another officer had been contaminated by statements made to him by his family. Now three members of ECPD were aware that a serious incident may have taken place and yet according to the reports, no one has contacted the watch commander or their immediate supervisor. They continued forward without supervision or direction of the command staff of the police department.

PARAGRAPH 6:

What training has officer Moore received in conducting internal affairs investigations? How many internal affairs investigations has officer Moore conducted? What training has Officer Moore received in conducting investigations of sexual assaults? How many sexual assault investigations has Officer Moore conducted?

It is my understanding that officer Moore has minimal police experience (less than 5 years) and that all his police time has been spent in patrol.

The paragraph states that the conversation that took place at the school was recorded.

The tape just starts up, there is no mention of time, date, location, or the parties present in the room. This is standard and the minimal accepted practice for recording an interview.

When the tape is turned on the alleged female victim can be heard crying and taking deep breaths. What was said prior to the recorder being turned on? Why is there no mention in the reports by Officers LaChapelle or Moore about conversation outside of what was recorded? Where are the notes of conversation that was not recorded? If there are no notes and there was conversation outside of what was recorded then this is a serious deviation from accepted interview techniques.

It appears that the recorder is being turned off and on. There is no mention as to why this is being done. Standard police practice dictates that a statement be made that the recorder is being turned off. The same practice also dictates that when the recorder is turned back on that the time, and who is present in the room is read into the recorder. At one point it is mentioned that the parties are moving to another room. The tape ends there with that statement. Did they go to another room? Was there conversation in that room? Why was it not recorded? Where are the notes from the officers indicating what was said?

During the taping one of the officers tells the alleged victim that her mother is not upset with her, that she is upset with Kennedy. This statement is a form of coercion, agree with my statement and mother will continue to be angry with Kennedy and not with you. The problem again is that you are not soliciting a true response from the person being interviewed, you are having them react to your statement.

The written report from LaChapelle on what was said by the victim's mother is abbreviated and not written in chronological order. This is totally unacceptable when writing a police report about a major incident.

Appendix C

On October 4, 1989 LaChapelle began his career as a police officer and joined as a member of the Police Officers Association.

On December 2, 1989, LaChapelle successfully graduated from Southwestern Police Academy. Prior to his graduation, LaChapelle rode four hours per day as an observer with a uniformed patrol officer.

On January 5, 1990, LaChapelle received competent ratings in all categories of his performance review, including the following comment:

> *"Officer LaChapelle presents a positive image, always arrives for work neat, clean and well groomed.*
>
> *Due to the limited ability of this officer to become involved in field operations; many areas are difficult to evaluate. But even with this limitation Officer LaChapelle made the best use of each day and shows a true desire to perform in his job. Overall he performed at a competent level."*

LaChapelle was assigned to the 3 p.m. shift, during which time he functioned as a second officer in a patrol car.

On April 5, 1990, LaChapelle received four competent ratings and an outstanding rating (the highest level) in his performance review. The following comment was included in his review:

> *"Officer LaChapelle has a strong foundation in police patrol procedures which he continues to build on. For the most part, his written work is neat and accurate and is seldom returned for additional work. He shows continual improvement in this area as he is exposed to more complex investigations.*
>
> *Officer LaChapelle has not missed any work due to illness or other causes during this rating period. He is consistently early and prepared for his shift. Officer LaChapelle gives maximum effort daily and keeps his mind on his*

job. One of his strong points is his positive energetic attitude. He seems to be very enthusiastic about his work and displays a strong attitude and interest. Officer LaChapelle works well with his peers. He maintains a neat and well groomed appearance while on duty. Officer LaChapelle is developing into a competent effective police officer. It is recommend that, he receive his next scheduled pay increase."

On July 4, 1990, LaChapelle received a satisfactory performance review, including outstanding marks in personal relations and he received a Class B Commendation. The review included many commending comments, including:

"LaChapelle is well liked and accepted by his peers. He is a team player and is always willing to assist officers in the field. He is responsible to supervision and receptive to criticism. He desires to improve in all facets of the job and his efforts to do so have been evident. He constantly stays busy, adheres to Department policy and Regulations, and has had 100% attendance during the rating period."

On July 19, 1990, LaChapelle received a letter of commendation.

On October 4, 1990, LaChapelle received a satisfactory performance review, including outstanding marks in work habits and personal relations.

LaChapelle also received a citizen's commendation for a presentation he made to El Cajon Summit High School. In this review, it was recommended that LaChapelle receive a merit increase in pay.

On October 26, 1990, LaChapelle received a letter of commendation for his work on a felony assault and battery investigation.

On January 4, 1991, LaChapelle received a satisfactory performance review, including highly satisfactory marks in quantity of work performed and personal relations.

On April 4, 1991, LaChapelle received a satisfactory performance review, including highly satisfactory marks" in understanding, thoroughness, written expression, responsiveness to supervision, getting along with fellow employees, and appropriate attire. LaChapelle also received a letter from the San Diego Child Protective Services praising him for his thorough and complete investigation on a certain case.

The review also recommended that LaChapelle be placed on permanent status as a police officer.

In April, 1990, LaChapelle was placed on permanent status.

In the summer of 1990, LaChapelle received two Class 3 Commendations: one for his self-initiated investigation of an assault with a deadly weapon case; and the other for his thorough crime scene investigation of a burglary.

On October 4, 1991, LaChapelle received a highly satisfactory performance review, including highly satisfactory marks in job understanding, job knowledge and skills, initiative in work improvement, amount of work performed, completion of work on schedule, accuracy of reports, thoroughness, written expression, exercises proper safety practices, complies with instructions, coordinating with others, responsiveness to supervision, and getting along with fellow employees.
The review also contained the following comments:

> *"During the last quarter, Officer LaChapelle has done a highly satisfactory job. He is enthusiastic and conscientious. He constantly looks for ways to improve. LaChapelle has a very good grasp of his responsibilities. He can be counted on to do a thorough and complete job on both assignments and self-initiated activity.*
>
> *On three occasions during this last quarter, LaChapelle. initiated contact with local probation schools in order to solve budding juvenile gang activity on his sector. Each time major problems were averted due largely to LaChapelle's ability to relate to youth groups.*
>
> *Officer LaChapelle is an asset to this department." The review also recommended that LaChapelle receive a pay increase.*

On or about November, 1991, LaChapelle involved himself during working hours and during his own time as a volunteer working with problem youth and gang members. He also volunteered his time to work at Summit High School with youth on probation in an effort to build their self esteem and respect for law enforcement.

For his work with problem youth in 1991 and 1992, LaChapelle received sixteen letters of appreciation and several Class C Commendations.

On October 4, 1992, LaChapelle received a highly satisfactory performance review, including highly satisfactory marks in job skills, quantity, quality, work habits, and personal relations categories. The review included the following comments:

> *"Officer LaChapelle's work is always completed in a timely manner and he generally conducts thorough investigations. His written work product is neat, legible and rarely returned for correction.*

Officer LaChapelle demonstrates good safety practices at all times. He plans and organizes his work in an effort to utilize his time in an efficient manner, complies with work instructions, works well with others and takes pride in his work performance. Officer LaChapelle is easy to supervise and is a respected member of his shift. He works well with the public demonstrating a friendly approach when making citizen contacts. He is always well groomed and neatly dressed. The review recommended that LaChapelle receive a pay increase.

In 1992, LaChapelle received the following awards for his efforts as a community leader and an exemplary police officer:

    a.   United Way of San Diego's Community Involvement Award;
    b.   San Diego County Probation Department's Community Involvement Award;
    c.   El Cajon Police Department's City of El Cajon Class "A" Commendation;
    d.   El Cajon Police Department's Police Star Award.

In January 1993, LaChapelle was assigned to Community Relations/Crime Analysis Division as School Liaison Officer. As School Liaison Officer, LaChapelle's duties included answering all calls for service at junior and senior high schools, providing high visibility patrol around school campuses, serving as liaison between school administrators and the El Cajon Police Department, and working with high risk youth.

On October 1993, LaChapelle received a highly satisfactory performance review, including an outstanding mark in the amount of work performed. The review included the following comments:

> *"Kevin has made great progress this year in reaching department goals and objectives. He has put forth significant effort toward implementing the*

School Liaison Program. Kevin has developed a reputation for being a dedicated and caring individual who is committed to improving the safety and learning environment of our campuses. He understands his role and has the necessary job knowledge and skills to be highly effective. Kevin demonstrates a genuine desire to improve his work product. He is extremely tenacious in the performance of his duties and completes a tremendous number of tasks in a timely manner.

In the past three months, Kevin has closed several major cases by arrest and has recovered several thousand dollars worth of property. Some of these cases include a carjacking, two strong arm robberies, several residential burglaries, stolen bike case, a child molest case and a series of school burglaries. When initiating an investigation, he follows up on leads through completion of the case. Much of his success can be attributed to information he receives from his contacts with youth from this community.

Officer LaChapelle is very conscientious in his work habits. He is a highly motivated individual who plans and organizes his work while coordinating well with others. Recently he has been assigned as the Serious Habitual Offender (SHO) coordinator to work with Crime Analysis in meeting grant objectives. He also works with gang detectives identifying local gang members and serves on San Diego County Task Force (TAGNET) to target taggers and gang members from the area.

Kevin gets along well with fellow employees and is very responsive to supervision. He possesses very good public relations skills and is always well groomed. He has received several letters of commendation from citizens and his immediate supervisor." The review also recommended that LaChapelle receive an increase in pay.

In 1993, LaChapelle received the following awards for his efforts as a community leader and an exemplary police officer:

a. *Law Enforcement Network's 1993 Officer of the Year;*
b. *El Cajon Police Department's city of El Cajon Class "A" Commendation;*
c. *San Diego County Board of Supervisor's Proclamation for Outstanding Commitment to Community Youth;*
d. *United Way of San Diego's 1993 community Hero Award;*

e. *United Way of San Diego's Golden Rule Award of 1993;*
f. *El Cajon Elks Lodge outstanding Service Award of 1993;*
g. *San Diego County Probation Department's community Involvement Award.*

When LaChapelle was assigned to School Liaison Officer in 1993, his immediate supervisor was Lt. "S".

In 1994, LaChapelle received the following awards for his efforts as a community leader and an exemplary police officer:

a. *El Cajon Police Department's Officer of the Year*
b. *El Cajon Police Department's City of El Cajon Class "A" Commendation*
c. *Channel 10 News' Leadership Award*
d. *San Diego County Juvenile Justice Commission's Certificate of Appreciation*
e. *I Love A Cop's 1994 Officer of the Year*
f. *El Cajon Rotary Club's 1994 Officer of the Year*
g. *El Cajon Exchange Club 1994 Officer of the Year*
h. *California Congress of Parents, Teachers, and Students' Honorary Service Award.*

On or about April 23, 1994, LaChapelle received information that Lt. "S"'s son (who had an adult son at the time) and an El Cajon Police Officer were having unlawful intercourse with minors. LaChapelle brought this information to the attention of the La Mesa Police Department.

Lt. "S"'s son and the El Cajon police officer were arrested, charged, and convicted. One of the victims was the daughter of Lt. "S"'s secretary.

After the allegations were brought out, Lt. "S"'s secretary was laid-off from' her position.

After her son pleaded guilty, Lt. "S" remained LaChapelle's immediate supervisor, notwithstanding the fact that as a direct consequence of LaChapelle's actions Lt. "S"'s son was convicted of a criminal offense. El Cajon Police Department did take any steps to transfer Lt. "S" from her position as LaChapelle's supervisor.

LaChapelle is informed and believes and based on such information and belief alleges that in retaliation for LaChapelle's whistle-blowing activities within the El Cajon Police Department Lt. "S" harbored ill feelings toward LaChapelle and caused a hostile work environment.

After LaChapelle identified his supervisor Lt. "S"'s son and a fellow El Cajon police officer in a rape case of two minors, LaChapelle was ridiculed by fellow officers in the presence of Lt. "S" for "turning on his fellow brother officers."

Lt. "S" nor EL CAJON POLICE took any action to prevent this from occurring; nor did they take any steps to stop it. Furthermore Lt. "S" engaged in conversation with LaChapelle's colleagues during work hours, degrading LaChapelle for his actions in her son's conviction and for his other whistle-blowing activities within the EL CAJON POLICE DEPARTMENT.

LaChapelle was exposed to incidents of' Lt. "S" staring him down or intimidating him while in the police station. While on duty, Lt. "S" told LaChapelle that he ruined her son's life and that LaChapelle prevented her son from ever becoming a regular police officer, which was her son's lifelong dream.

Prior to his election to the Grossmont union High School Governing Board ("School Board") in November 1994, LaChapelle was intimidated by Lt. "S" to not run for School Board. This was a clear violation of Government Code § 3302 and Labor Code 1102.5.

Thereafter, LaChapelle was informed that he was "making waves in the Department" and because of his recent election to the school board, he would be losing his position as School Liaison Officer, which was somehow a "conflict of interest," and that he should put in for a transfer for an Alcohol Beverage Control. (ABC) assignment. This was a clear violation of Government Code § 3302 and Labor Code §§ 1.10, 1102, and 1102.5.

It was represented by Lt. "S" and the new EL CAJON POLICE ADMINISTRATION that ABC would conduct alcohol education to the schools for students and position would be available for LaChapelle's taking.

In addition, LaChapelle saw a notice posted by EL CAJON in the police station at the entry of the men's locker room, which stated that the ABC position was educational in nature and would be assigned to the Community Relations Division. The notice stated that one additional officer would be used to write citations for alcohol violations, such as selling alcohol to minors.

LaChapelle was specifically told that his DARE training would be an asset for this position, as it would be beneficial for an educational position, which fell into LaChapelle's expertise. It was made clear to LaChapelle that the ABC position would not require him in any way to be involved any undercover duty. In fact, other El Cajon police officers stated they did not apply for the ABC position because of its preventative/educational nature, as well as it being assigned to the community Relations Division, and that it was not an undercover assignment.

The ABC assignment was the result of a State of California grant received by EL CAJON.

LaChapelle was told that if he did not put in for this position he would end up on graveyard shift patrol, which would not allow him to continue his area of expertise in the juvenile justice system.

After LaChapelle applied for and accepted the ABC assignment, he was told that now the position was going to be an undercover vice enforcement type position, and that it soon would be transferring to the Crime Suppression unit under the direction of supervisor Lt. "S"'s husband, Sergeant "C" "S".

In his new position, plaintiff would be forced to frequent bars where prostitution and cigarette smoke were prevalent. LaChapelle was also told to drink alcoholic beverages to fit into his undercover role. Lt. "S", and the NEW EL CAJON POLICE ADMIN-ISTRATION knew that this conflicted with LaChapelle's religious beliefs and that this was not the type of position he applied for pursuant to the ABC grant.

LaChapelle was also subjected to an undercover assignment, working undercover in San Diego topless establishments without his consent or prior knowledge, including being solicited by prostitutes.

LaChapelle is informed and believes and based on such information and belief alleges that all of these things were done to LaChapelle to harass him because of his religious belief and to punish him for his whistle blowing activities, and to create an environment where he would have no alternative but to resign. In addition, Lt. "S" and the

NEW EL CAJON POLICE ADMINISTRATION also knew of LaChapelle's serious allergies to second hand cigarette smoke.

When LaChapelle complained of the work conditions to Lt. "S" and the NEW EL CAJON POLICE ADMINISTRATION he was ridiculed and told that he would be transferred to graveyard shift patrol or fired if he did not continue in this undercover position.

Consequently, LaChapelle suffered severe sinus problems as a result of the allergy to cigarette smoke. LaChapelle was transferred to a patrol assignment from Thursday— Saturday from 6:30 p.m.—7:00 a.m. which Lt. "S" knew prohibited him from fulfilling his obligation as an elected member of the School board, which met every other Thursday at 6:00 p.m.

When LaChapelle informed Lt. "S" and the NEW EL CAJON POLICE ADMIN-ISTRATION of the conflict, LaChapelle was told that his first responsibility was his police officer position and that EL CAJON POLICE did not have to accommodate him for a School Board meeting.

LaChapelle is informed and believes based on such information and belief alleges that Lt. "S" and the NEW EL CAJON POLICE ADMINSTRATION specifically sched-uled LaChapelle to work on Thursday nights so he could not attend his meetings at the School Board and to either cause him to resign or create the circumstances whereby he could be fired. In addition, LaChapelle is informed and believes and based on such information and belief alleges that Lt. "S" and the NEW EL CAJON POLICE ADMINISTRATION would look into the hostile working environment in which LaChapelle had to work. Lt. "S" was kept in her supervisory position over LaChapelle.

LaChapelle was forced into resigning from his position as a highly decorated police officer of six years.

978-0-595-38238-5
0-595-38238-X